FRANCIS SUAREZ

ON THE VARIOUS KINDS OF DISTINCTIONS

(*DISPUTATIONES METAPHYSICAE*, *Disputatio VII, de variis distinctionum generibus*)

Translation from the Latin,
with an introduction,

By

CYRIL VOLLERT, S.J., S.T.D.

MARQUETTE UNIVERSITY PRESS
MILWAUKEE, WISCONSIN

Mediæval Philosophical Texts in Translation

No. 4

MARQUETTE
UNIVERSITY

PRESS

MEDIÆVAL PHILOSOPHICAL TEXTS IN TRANSLATION No. 4

© 2007 Marquette University Press
Milwaukee, Wisconsin 53201-3141
All rights reserved.
www.marquette.edu/mupress/

First printing © 1947
Second printing © 1976
Third printing © 2007
Fourth printing © 2013

ISBN-10: 0-87462-204-2
ISBN-13: 978-087462-204-1

www.marquette.edu/mupress

MARQUETTE UNIVERSITY PRESS
MILWAUKEE

The Association of Jesuit University Presses

FRANCIS SUAREZ *ON THE VARIOUS KINDS OF DISTINCTIONS*

INTRODUCTION

THE reason for including Suarez in a series of texts on mediaeval philosophy is apparent. Suarez is the channel through which the Scholasticism of the Middle Ages passed to the modern world. Although he belongs to the Renaissance, his philosophy breathes the spirit of the Schoolmen. His *Disputationes metaphysicae* is the last great achievement of scholastic philosophy.

Life and Works

Francis Suarez, known as the *Doctor Eximius* ever since Benedict XIV conferred this honorary title on him, was born at Granada in Spain on January 5, 1548. At the age of thirteen he was sent to Salamanca to study canon law. His first request for admission into the Society of Jesus was refused: he was judged deficient in health and in talent. But in 1564, after insistent pleading, he was accepted.

In the beginning his endeavors to learn philosophy met with scant success. But by the end of the first year knowledge had made its bloody entrance; the new science yielded to his stubborn efforts, and he became marked as one of the better students. From 1566 to 1570 he studied theology at Salamanca. He taught philosophy for four years, and then theology for ten years at Segovia, Valladolid, and Rome. For reasons of health, he returned to Spain, and lectured in the schools at Alcalá, Salamanca, and Coimbra. The twenty-year professorship at the latter university was broken by his residence in Rome from 1603 to 1606. He died on September 25, 1617, in Lisbon, having reached his seventieth year.

Up to the age of forty-two, although he had been teaching philosophy and theology for some nineteen years, Suarez had not published a single page. In 1590 appeared the first of his long series of works, *De Incarnatione Verbi*. This was followed by *De mysteriis vitae Christi*, in 1592; *De sacramentis*, I, in 1595; *Disputationes metaphysicae*, two volumes, in 1597; *Varia opuscula theologica*, in 1599; *De sacramentis*, II, in 1602; *De censuris*, in 1603; *De Deo Uno et Trino*, in 1606; *De virtute et statu religionis*, vol. I, in 1608, vol. II, in 1609; *De legibus*, in 1612; and the *Defensio fidei catholicae*, in 1613. All of these Suarez saw through the press himself. After his death were published: *De gratia*, I and III, in 1619; *De angelis*, 1620; *De opere sex dierum*, and *De anima*, 1621; *De fide, spe, et caritate*, 1621; *De virtute et statu religionis*, vol. III, in 1624, and vol. IV, in 1625; *De ultimo fine*, etc., in 1628; *De gratia, II,* in 1651; and *De vera intelligentia auxilii efficacis*, in 1655. Finally, a volume called *Opuscula sex inedita* appeared in 1859. Material sufficient to fill four more folio volumes still lies buried in manuscripts.

The quality, profundity, and amplitude of these works have gained for Suarez the renown of being, after St. Thomas Aquinas, the "most scholastic of the Scholastics."[1]

Philosophical Thought in the Age of Suarez

To understand Suarez and appreciate his position in the history of thought, we must recall that he did not live in the Golden Age of Scholasticism, but during a time of turmoil and radical readjustments which wound up the mediaeval order and ushered in the modern world. The career of St. Thomas coincided with a period during which metaphysical activity was hastening toward its glorious climax. Suarez came at a time when Catholicism was under attack, and when the general intellectual bias was not in the direction of metaphysics. To defend the Church, he drew upon the amassed treasures of scholastic thought. But he saw that if Scholasticism were to be revived, it had to be presented in a form more in keeping with the preoccupations and awareness of his century. To reach the intellectual leaders of his day, he had to bring the metaphysics of St. Thomas down to the level of their blunter minds. No less than Aquinas, he is the representative of an epoch.

Scholasticism had been in decline since the fourteenth century. It gradually lost its intellectual vigor and its predominance in Western civilization. It no longer permeated the thought processes of the European mind. But it clung tenaciously to what life it had, and refused to relinquish its heritage to the encroachments of new ideas.

In the sixteenth century a brilliant, though not lasting, revival of Scholasticism flared up. The movement was chiefly theological. Its inspiration was mainly reaction against the Reformation. Under the stimulus of the Council of Trent, it chose to deal mostly with questions occasioned by the heresies of the times.

Parallel with the theological movement went a philosophical restoration, characterized by a return to the thirteenth century, above all to the thought of St. Thomas. This resurgence reached its crest in Spain, which had not as yet completely broken clear of the Middle Ages and which, partly for geographical reasons, partly owing to the spirit and culture of its people, was less shaken by the tempest of the Reformation and less charmed by the Renaissance than the rest of Europe.

Salamanca was the starting point and remained the center of the philosophical revival. Since 1524 Francis de Vittoria had been laboring

---

[1] Z. Gonzalez, O. P., *Historia de la Filosofia* (Madrid, 1878), II, 540.

heroically for the establishment of a new and more vital Thomistic school. Soon his fame and that of the university filled Spain, and the movement sped to Alcalá and to Coimbra, as well as to Italy, though in somewhat diminished vigor.

The works produced by Vittoria's fellow-Dominicans, Melchior Cano, Dominic Soto, and later by Dominic Bañez, were mainly of the nature of commentaries on the *Summa theologica,* which had replaced the *Sentences* of Peter Lombard as the basic treatise in the schools. But before long the commentary gave way to more independent essays and systematic works that allowed ampler scope for personal exposition and development.

To this resurgence of Scholasticism the scholars of the newly-founded Society of Jesus, established in Spain about 1548, gave whole-hearted support. St. Ignatius, while still a student at the University of Paris, had greatly admired the teaching of St. Thomas, and later appointed him as the official doctor of his new Order. Thus the philosophical bent of the Jesuits veered toward Thomism. However, since the Society had no direct roots in the mediaeval tradition, and was not bound by fraternal ties to the *Doctor Communis,* it was freer to heed an original urge in philosophical speculation.

When the century was well along appeared Francis Suarez, who was to occupy in the Society of Jesus an eminence similar to that of St. Thomas among the Dominicans, and of Duns Scotus among the Franciscans.

The Place of Suarez in Philosophy

To indicate the place of Suarez in philosophy by heaping encomium upon encomium would be a superfluous and tedious task.[2] But even allowing for the exaggeration inseparable from effusive compliment, the rank of Suarez as theologian, philosopher, and jurist is high in the judgment of sober and competent critics. In Scheeben's opinion Suarez is the "most prolific of all later Scholastics, distinguished alike by clarity, conservatism, depth, and copiousness".[3] According to Grabmann, the *Disputationes metaphysicae* is a monumental achievement of scholastic philosophy, and of philosophical speculation in general, a frequent guidepost to truth, a work plotted on a grand scale and independent in design. He adds that we must experience a certain shame that we can point to no such com-

---

[2] Samples of laudatory appraisals, some florid, some graceful, some sincere and obective, have been gathered by R. de Scorraille, *Francois Suarez,* 2 vols. (Paris: Lethielleux, 1912-13), II, 431-40, and by H. Hurter, *Nomenclator literarius,* 3d. ed., 5 vols. (Oeniponte: Libraria Academica Wagneriana, 1903-13), III, 379 f. Suarez is "the new Augustine," "the Thomas of his century," and "the universal doctor of these latter ages."

[3] M. J. Scheeben, *Handbuch der katholischen Dogmatik,* 3 vols. (Freiburg im Breisgau: Herder, 1873-87), I, 451.

prehensive, profound, and original metaphysics in Neo-Scholasticism.[4] Elsewhere the same critic remarks that the *Disputationes metaphysicae* is the most carefully worked-out system of metaphysics ever to come from the pen of a Catholic philosopher, and finds that the work is characterized by a full discussion of problems and their solutions, great intimacy with preceding Scholasticism, and tranquil objectivity.[5] Bernareggi, after reiterating the sentiment that Suarez was the St. Thomas of his time, continues: "If he failed to unify all as did St. Thomas, at least he assembled, mastered, and clarified all that previous scholars had bequeathed to his century."[6]

Enthusiastic Suarezians like to repeat the benevolent judgment of Z. Gonzalez, O.P., that, after St. Thomas, Suarez is perhaps the most eminent personification of scholastic philosophy, and that, again after St. Thomas, his conception of philosophy is the most complete, universal, and solid we possess.[7] Very reasonable, and surely acceptable to all, is McCormick's verdict. He points out that during the era of commentators which came after Albert, Thomas, and Scotus, Suarez refused to accept the view that scholastic thought had crystallized, and approached philosophy with a new spirit, eventually becoming the supreme influence in a revival of Scholasticism, and producing what remains, even to our own day, the last notable treatise on Scholastic metaphysics.[8]

Perhaps the last word that can be said at the present time has been uttered by Rast: "Preliminary to an appraisal of the philosophy or theology of Suarez, detailed monographs on the most important parts of his system are needed. How jejune is the literature on this subject, a glance at the bibliography given in Ueberweg will show. To do justice to the Spaniard, who is the center of so much controversy, and to assign him his rightful place in the history of philosophy and theology, thorough researches must also be made into his relations with his predecessors and his influence on later thinkers."[9]

Influence

Despite the lack of such studies, enough is known of the success of the *Disputationes metaphysicae* to enable us to surmise the magnitude

---

[4] M. Grabmann, "Die Disputationes metaphysicae des Franz Suarez in ihrer methodischen Eigenart und Fortwirken," in *Mittelalterliches Geistesleben*, 2 vols. (München: Max Hueber, 1926-36), I 559.

[5] *Geschichte der katholischen Theologie* (Freiburg i. B: Herder, 1933), p. 169.

[6] A. Bernareggi, "La personlita scientifica di Francesco Suarez," in A. Gemelli (ed.), *Scritti vari pubblicati in occasione del terzo centenario della morte di Francesco Suarez* (Milano, 1918), p. 31.

[7] Thus, among others, E. Masterson. "Are the Metaphysics of Suarez in Opposition to Those of St. Thomas?" *Irish Ecclesiastical Record* XXIII (1924), p. 54.

[8] I. F. McCormick, "The Significance of Suarez for a Revival of Scholasticism," in C. A. Hart (ed.), *Aspects of the New Scholastic Philosophy* (New York: Benziger, 1932), p. 33 f.

[9] M. Rast, "Die Possibilienlehre des Franz Suarez," *Scholastik*, X (1935), p. 340.

of the influence Suarez exercised. The bulky work, exceeding two thousand folio pages in double columns, ran through twenty editions within a few years of its publication. Ueberweg records that Spanish Scholasticism, especially as represented by Suarez, was widespread both in Catholic and in Protestant universities. A. Heerebord calls Suarez the "pope and prince of all metaphysicians;" he complains that Spanish Scholasticism has invaded the Protestant schools, and remarks that all the manuals of philosophy of that period are nothing but imitations of the *Disputationes* of Suarez.[10] The philosopher, Joachim Jungius, studied Suarez in Rostock at the beginning of the seventeenth century; and his biographer, S. Guhrauer, writes that in the Protestant universities of the time the metaphysical works of Suarez enjoyed the popularity formerly reserved to the treatises of Melanchthon.[11] K. Eschweiler emphasizes the astounding and widespread influence of Suarezianism during the seventeenth century, a period during which Thomism remained alive only in small and isolated circles.[12] He notes that whenever a sample is taken of the philosophical literature current in the German universities from about 1620 to 1690, the metaphysics of the Suarezian school is invariably found to be the favorite philosophy.[13]

Descartes was accustomed to carry about with him on his travels the *Summa theologica* of St. Thomas and the *Disputationes metaphysicae* of Suarez. Spinoza was well acquainted with the philosophy of Suarez, although, very likely, only at second hand. Leibnitz narrates that as a boy he read the later Scholastics with pleasure, and remarks with some complacency that he had progressed so far he could read Suarez with as great facility as people generally read novels.[14] Schopenhauer cites Suarez frequently; he esteemed the *Disputationes metaphysicae* as a "true compendium of Scholasticism," and "an authentic compendium of the whole of scholastic wisdom."[15]

After Schopenhauer, the prestige of Suarez among non-scholastic philosophers began to wane. But in Catholic circles he still generally remains, though far behind St. Thomas, the most influential of the great

10 Cf. *Friedrich Ueberwegs Grundriss der Geschichte de Philosophie,* 12th ed., 5 vols. (Berlin: E. S. Mittler & Sohn, 1923-28), III, 214 f.; J. Maréchal, *Précis d'histoire de la philosophie moderne,* I (Louvain: Museum Lessianum, 1933), p. 113.
11 Ueberweg, *ibid.,* p. 215; Grabmann, *Mittelalterliches Geistesleben,* I, 538. Grabmann lists a number of similar testimonies, pp. 536, 538 f.
12 K. Eschweiler, "Die Philosophie der spanischen Spätscholastik auf den deutschen Universitäten des siebzehnten Jahrhunderts," in H. Finke (ed.), *Gesammelte Aufsätze zur Kulturgeschichte Spaniens.* Erst Reihe (Münster in Westfalen: Aschendorff, 1928), p. 283.
13 *Ibid.,* p. 311.
14 Maréchal, *op. cit.,* pp. 62, 113, 155.
15 *Sämtliche Werke,* III, 20 and IV, 70; quoted by Grabmann, *op. cit.,* p. 535.

scholastic metaphysicians; and in Spain and the countries of Latin America he has lost little of his former ascendancy.

The Metaphysical Disputations

The two large folio volumes of the *Disputationes metaphysicae* appeared in Salamanca in 1597. In his brief foreword, "Ad lectorem," Suarez indicates his reason for undertaking this project: "It is impossible for anyone to become a competent theologian unless he builds upon a solid metaphysical foundation." He develops this view in the *Prooemium* or prologue to his work. The science of metaphysics, he holds, is indispensable for a mastery of theology. More intimately than any other human field of knowledge, it is connected with theology; it has for its object the most universal and supreme principles which embrace all being and are the foundation of all knowledge. This function of metaphysics was for Suarez a compelling motive for interrupting his theological labors and producing, in one systematic, comprehensive work, the results of his metaphysical studies and investigations, begun many years before. The prologue reads as follows:

"Sacred and supernatural theology relies on divine illumination and on principles revealed by God. However, it is cultivated by human reasoning and investigation, and therefore enlists the aid of truths naturally known, using them as ministers and instruments to develop its deductions and to illustrate divine truths. But of all the natural sciences, that which holds the primacy and has won the name of first philosophy is most valuable for promoting sacred and supernatural theology. For among them all it approaches most closely to the science of divine things, and also explains and vindicates those natural principles which embrace the universe of being and in one way or another stand at the basis of all learning.

"For this reason I wished to revise and expand what I have worked out for my students and publicly taught on various occasions during many years concerning this natural wisdom, so that the results of my reflections might be made available to the general public. Accordingly I am forced for a time to interrupt, or rather to postpone, the more weighty commentaries and disputations on sacred theology I am so busily engaged in, as well as the taxing labor required for their publication.

"It often happened that while I was treating of divine mysteries, metaphysical problems would come up. Without a knowledge and understanding of these, the higher mysteries of Christianity can scarcely, if at all, be discussed as they deserve. Hence I had to mingle baser questions with supernatural subjects, a practice that is annoying to readers and is not very profitable for them; or else, to avoid this awkward procedure, I had briefly to propose my own opinion in such matters, and

[6]

thus demand of my readers a blind faith in my judgment. This was embarrassing for me, and could well seem out of place to them. Metaphysical principles and truths are so closely interwoven with theological conclusions and deductions, that if knowledge and full understanding of the former are lacking, knowledge of the latter must necessarily suffer.

"Led on by such considerations, I yielded to repeated requests and decided to write the present work. I have arranged all the metaphysical disputations according to a method calculated to combine comprehensive treatment with brevity, and so to be of greater service to revealed wisdom. Hence it will not be necessary to divide the work into several books. For all that pertains to this doctrine and is suitable to its subject matter in the light of the method adopted, can be fully handled in a limited number of disputations. What belongs to "pure philosophy" or dialectics has, so far as possible, been left out as not in keeping with the scope of the work. I shall adhere to this norm, even though I am aware that other writers on metaphysics devote much space to such subjects. But before I begin to treat of the subject-matter of this doctrine I shall, God willing, discuss wisdom or metaphysics itself, its object, use, necessity and its attributes and rewards."

The work falls into two main parts, coinciding with the two volumes in which it was published. It comprises fifty-four disputations in all. The first volume treats of metaphysics in its broadest comprehension: being as such, and the properties and causes of being. The first disputation deals with the object of metaphysics; the second inaugurates an exposition of the concept of being. Disputations III to XI discuss the passions and transcendental properties of being. Disputations XII to XXVII embody the author's doctrine on causes.

The second volume opens with a consideration of infinite and finite being. Two disputations deal with natural knowledge of the existence, nature, and attributes of God. The remaining disputations are devoted to the metaphysics of finite being, distributed according to the Aristotelian categories.

As the title indicates, the work is cast in the form of disputations. The discussions follow a regular pattern. First, the problem is stated. Then the various solutions that have actually been proposed by philosophers are reviewed *(Variae opiniones)*. Thirdly, Suarez gives what he considers to be the true doctrine or, as the case may be, the most probable theory *(Vera sententia* or *Resolutio quaestionis)*. A refutation of opposing views often brings the disputation to a close.

Method

The procedure followed by Suarez is a development of the dialectical method so popular in mediaeval Scholasticism, but differs from it in many

[7]

ways. The manner of presentation he evolved reflects his dissatisfaction both with the arrangement of Aristotle's *Metaphysics* and with the philosophical treatises of his predecessors.

Suarez had a low opinion of Aristotle's procedure. He complained that the Stagirite "had little sense of method or definite order, and apparently poured forth his thoughts as they came to his mind."[16] He was aware of other deficiencies in Aristotle's work, as, for instance, that Book II raises many questions that are never taken up and answered, and that Book XI contains little beyond superfluous repetitions. Hence he decided to break away from Aristotle's text.

But he could find no satisfactory model in the writings of earlier Scholastics. There was no dearth of systematic treatises, but in these works theology and philosophy were usually unfolded side by side and intermingled. In the field of philosophy as such there were many short works and *opuscula,* such as the *De ente et essentia* of St. Thomas, but these could furnish no exemplar for the mammoth project Suarez contemplated. The numberless commentaries on Aristotle displayed as little order as their original. More to the point was the growing "Question literature," wherein philosophers treated new problems not contained in the text that served as the basis of their commentaries, although the questions were in some fashion suggested by the topics treated in the text. As this genre developed, reference to the text tended more and more to vanish, and logical arrangement according to subject matter became more common.

Suarez made the final step, entirely suppressing the textual basis and arranging the vast subject matter of metaphysics according to an organic and carefully integrated plan. Thus he has the distinction of being the first to present scholastic metaphysics in a complete, systematic treatise.

His method, the climax of a long evolution, is always substantially the same. He gives exact information as to researches thus far made on the problem under discussion, tells who has written on it, what his principles were, and to what conclusions he came. In thus presenting the state of the question, he gives a faithful record of the pertinent literature, and generally offers a true history of the problem. Indeed, his careful and dispassionate review of the many opinions he discovered has merited for him the honor of being the first historian of Scholasticism. Discussion of the abundant material so painstakingly collected then leads him on to his own conclusion, which he endeavors to substantiate with series upon series of arguments. He could not limit himself to mere repetition of the theories of others, nor accept any doctrine for the

---

[16] Introduction to "Liber tertius metaphysicae" in the "Index locupletissimus," Vivès ed., XXV, ix.

sole reason that it had been advocated by authoritative doctors. In this honest independence, at least, he proved himself a true disciple of St. Thomas, who had never followed any author with slavish submission, but had always looked for truth wherever it might be.

The exposition and criticism of the various theories reviewed are for Suarez but a means for the formulation of his own judgment and for the construction of his metaphysical system. The charge of "eclecticism" often hurled at him by those who do not agree with his teaching is hardly justified in the sense of a reproach. Undoubtedly Suarez is one of the most eclectic of philosophers. But, as Grabmann points out, his is a sound eclecticism, not such as superficially borrows ideas from different systems and ranges them together in mechanical fashion. It is an eclecticism that critically tests all theories, whether ancient or modern, and assembles the conclusions reached into an organic whole.[17] Bernareggi also finds that the eclectic synthesis of Suarez, like that of St. Thomas, is organic, and marked by solidity and doctrinal coherence.[18] Grabmann does not hesitate to call eclecticism the "great basic methodological principle of the *Philosophia perennis*."[19] Most historians of philosophy would agree with Pelster that inductive habits of thought are a valuable check on sheer deduction, and that all knowledge here on earth results from the gradual accretion of separate perceptions of truth. "Suarez was an eclectic in much the way that Thomas was."[20]

In his enthusiastic fashion Grabmann states that the great length and complexity of procedure with which Suarez develops metaphysical problems do not lead to confusion. The exposition is clear, he writes, the relation of question to question is shown, the core of the problem and the root of the difficulty are uncovered, the historico-critical review of previous theories and their principles is carefully made, and the philosopher's own solution of the problem is unfolded in its genesis. The austere objectivity of the procedure, Grabmann adds, reminds one of St. Thomas, although in brevity and precision Suarez is inferior to Thomas.[21]

Much of this is well said. An antidote against possible exaggeration is supplied by Astrain. Greater clarity in Suarez' method of composition could be desired, he asserts. Some confusion is engendered by excessively detailed presentation of the opinions of adversaries. Not only does Suarez report the many theories at great length but, in his passion for fairness, after proposing his own views, he gives his opponents another chance to urge their arguments. At times he enters so deeply into

[17] *Mittelalterliches Geistesleben*, I, 548.
[18] *Art. cit., Scritti vari,* p. 31.
[19] *Op. cit.,* p. 559.
[20] F. Pelster, *Scholastik*, I (1926), p. 145
[21] *Op. cit.,* p. 536.

their minds that he bolsters up their case with arguments of his own, even speaking in the first person. In consequence, the reader may be hard put to it to determine which is the position of Suarez and which is that of his adversaries. The resulting bewilderment can be overcome only by a patient rereading and re-examination of the whole course of the development.[22]

Sources

Notwithstanding his independence and originality, Suarez is deeply indebted to his predecessors. He is, after all, heir to two thousand years of philosophical thinking. A bare enumeration of the authors he has studied at first hand would cover several pages.[23]

Of the ancients, Aristotle of course influenced him most. Suarez was also well acquainted with the works of Themistius, Alexander of Aphrodisias, Simplicius, Ammonius, and John Philoponus, all of them Greek commentators on Aristotle. His mastery of Platonic literature exceeded that of mediaeval philosophers. He cites Plotinus, Plutarch, Proclus, and Boethius.

His knowledge of Scholasticism from its beginnings in St. Anselm, through its transitional period in William of Auxerre, and down to his own day is extensive and detailed. He knew the school of Albert the Great only in Albert himself, as the works of Albert's disciples remained unprinted and so were not readily available. Unquestionably he knew the Thomistic school best of all: Hervaeus Natalis and Peter Paludanus among the earlier Thomists; John Capreolus, Paul Soncinas, and Dominic of Flanders from the fifteenth century; Chrysostom Javelli, Cajetan, Francis Sylvester Ferrariensis, Conrad Köllin, Diego of Astudillo,[24] Dominic Soto, Bartholomew of Medina, and others from the sixteenth century. The Franciscan school is represented by Alexander of Hales, St. Bonaventure, and Richard of Mediavilla. Scarcely a problem is treated by Suarez without reference to Duns Scotus. Among the older Scotists he cites Francis de Mayronis, Andreas Andreae, and John of Bassolis; among the later Scotists, Anthony Trombeta, Lychetus of Brescia, and Andrew Vega. The name of Henry of Ghent appears frequently. Of the Aegidian school Suarez knows Giles of Rome, Thomas of Strasburg, and Gregory of Rimini. Durandus and Peter Aureoli represent the precursors of nominalism. Of the nominalistic school itself

---

[22] A. Astrain, *Historia de la Compañia de Jesús en la Asistencia de España,* 7 vols. (Madrid: Razón y Fe, 1912-25), IV, 64.

[23] For a partial list, see Grabmann, *op. cit., pp.* 532-5. The summary that follows omits many names. It likewise omits all references to the Fathers, of whom Suarez possessed a knowledge scarcely less extensive than that of Petavius.

[24] Referred to as "Astudil" by Suarez. The name is not listed in Hurter, *Nomenclator literarius.* He is Fray Diego de Astudillo, a Spanish Dominican from the village of Astudillo, which is "un población de Palencia en Castilla la Vieja." He wrote commentaries on Aristotle, especially on the *Physica.*

Suarez knows Ockham, Marsilius of Inghen, Albert of Saxony, Adam Wodeham, John Mayor, and Gabriel Biel.

Suarez had read the chief exponents of the Arabian and Jewish philosophy that so greatly influenced Scholasticism. He was also acquainted with Latin Averroism as represented by John of Janduno, Paul of Venice, Cajetan of Thiene, Augustine Niphus, and others. He knew Renaissance philosophy in the writings of Marsilius Ficinus, Pico della Mirandola, and Julius Serenius of Brescia.

Finally, among his fellow-Jesuits Francis Toletus, Peter Fonseca, the "Aristotle of Coimbra," and the latter's collaborators on the *Cursus Conimbricensium* profoundly influenced Suarez. On occasion he cites his great contemporary, St. Robert Bellarmine.

It goes without saying that Suarez is indebted most of all to St. Thomas, whom he follows in many questions of paramount importance. But he disagrees with Aquinas, although reverently, in a number of basic theses. He denies a real distinction between essence and existence in created beings, he thinks that prime matter may be capable of existence in its own right without the determining and actuating influence of substantial form, he departs from St. Thomas in his teaching on the principle of individuation and in his theory of knowledge.

What, then, are the relations between St. Thomas and Suarez? Non-Thomists are inclined to classify Suarez as a Thomist. Strict Thomists insist that he is nothing of the sort. Obviously, the solution must take as its starting point the establishment of a norm for determining what Thomism is. If the essence of Thomist philosophy is adequately represented by the celebrated "twenty-four theses," approved by the Sacred Congregation of Studies as reflecting the true mind of St. Thomas,[25] Suarez can hardly be considered a Thomist in any proper sense. He questions, modifies, or rejects most of these propositions. Placed as he was midstream between two opposing currents, the Thomist and the Scotist, Suarez favored now the Dominicans, now the Franciscans, and often struck out boldly on his own. Intellectually he had, perhaps, more of the critical spirit of Scotus than of the metaphysical acumen of Aquinas.

The divergence of Suarez from St. Thomas in no way implies that there is not a wealth of carefully reasoned and sound philosophy in the massive volumes of the Spanish scholar.[26] By his method, his recourse to primary sources, and his originality of speculation, he contributed substantially to the advancement of philosophy. The evaluation Grabmann set upon his work remains just: the *Disputationes metaphysicae* consti-

---

[25] Cf. *Acta Apostolicae Sedis*, VI (1914), 383-6.
[26] For a survey of the metaphysical, psychological, and juristic thought of Suarez, see Ueberweg, III, 211-4.

tutes the most detailed, copious, and complete systematization of meta-physics in existence.[27]

The Seventh Disputation

Disputation VII has been chosen as a sample of the metaphysics of Suarez for two reasons. First, it is typical both of his method and of his philosophical thought; many of his characteristic doctrines are briefly treated in it, or at least are indicated. Secondly, it introduces his teaching on the modes, without which much of his philosophy is unintelligible, and above all propounds his theory on distinctions, a point of capital importance for a grasp of Suarezian metaphysics. As the views of Suarez on distinctions and modes are clearly brought out in the Disputation itself, there seems to be no need of a preliminary exposition of these tenets in survey form.[28]

Suarez treats of distinctions in the context of his discussion on the unity of being, Disputations IV to VII. Disputation IV deals with *unum* in general, Disputation V with individual unity and the principle of individuation, Disputation VI with universals, and Disputation VII with the various kinds of distinctions. The connection between the question of unity and that of distinctions is explained by Suarez himself in the introduction to Disputation VII. Section 3 of this Disputation, on "the same" and "other," is added to the treatise on distinctions in order to round out the general discussion of unity.

The main reason why a philosopher's theory of distinctions is important is that his solution to the problem of distinctions is a key to his concept of being. For distinctions are based on the nature of being; therefore a metaphysician's view of the nature of distinctions leads to an understanding of his doctrine of being itself.[29] In reading Disputation VII, the student can profitably ponder whether any ideas developed in it support the suggestion put forth by a scholar of our own day, who is both a profound philosopher and a shrewd appraiser of intellectual trends:

> Everything is accounted for if we recall that Suarez lived in a nominalistic milieu, and that, despite his avowed reaction in favor of realism in logic, he did not fully succeed in keeping his meta-physics free from this influence.[30]

---

[27] *Op. cit.*, p. 535.
[28] A sufficiently detailed account of these two questions may be found in P. E. Nolan, "The Suarezian Modes," *Proceedings of the Tenth Annual Convention of the Jesuit Educational Association* (Chicago: Loyola U. Press, 1931), pp. 184-200.
[29] This point has been fully discussed by Michael V. Murray, S.J., in his hitherto unpublished doctoral dissertation, *The Theory of Distinctions in the Metaphysics of Francis Suarez*, Fordham University, 1944. Dr. Murray advances cogent reasons, well fortified by historical research, for his conclusion that Suarez was thoroughly imbued with the widespread nominalism of his time.
[30] J. Maréchal, *Le point de départ de la métaphysique*, I (2d. ed., Louvain: Museum Lessianum, 1927), p. 185.

Indispensable, too, for an appreciation of Suarezian metaphysics, is his modal theory. Suarez perceived that most things are highly complex, composed as they are of distinct entities, substantial and accidental. Hence he concluded that their essential union is tenuous, or even impossible, without some ultimate bond. This bond is a mode of being. He saw, further, that every created being is subject to numberless determinations which lie outside its essence, but do not contribute new reality to it. The mode supplies the complement of finality. It closes and terminates an essence; it is not a formal, but a completing act.

The Suarezian system is coherent in its complicated structure. Suarez remains faithful to his primary concepts of entity, unity, existence, and distinction, and traces out their implications to the ultimate conclusion. No greater mistake could be made than to attempt to "purify" the system by suppressing the modes. Take away the modes, and the Suarezian structure collapses; just as, in his view, without the unifying function of the modes, finite beings themselves would fall apart. Whether for a mind craving for reality the modes provide satisfying fare, is another question. A study of Disputation VII should help toward an answer.

Bibliography

This bibliographical note is limited to a few references. A rather elaborate bibliography has been compiled by C. C. Riedl in *Jesuit Thinkers of the Renaissance*, to be listed below. This book is presumably available to most readers of the present text.

A complete, critical edition of the works of Suarez, measuring up to modern standards, has never been issued. Such an edition will ultimately appear in the series, "Societatis Iesu Selecti Scriptores." No information is forthcoming as to when publication may be expected to begin. For a history of editions of the works of Suarez, the reader is referred to C. Sommervogel, S.J., *Bibliothèque de la Compagnie de Jésus*, 9 vols. (Paris: Alphonse Picard, 1890-1900), VII, 1661-87; IX, 867 f. The latest of the complete editions is *Opera Omnia*, 26 vols. (Paris: Vivès, 1856-66; some sets are dated 1856-77) and 2 vols. of indices (1878). The *Disputationes metaphysicae* are contained in vols. XXV and XXVI. The translation of Disputation VII is based on the text in this edition.

The standard biography is that of R. de Scorraille, S.J., *François Suarez de la Compagnie de Jésus*, 2 vols. (Paris: Lethielleux, 1912-13); a critical appraisal of previous biographies is given in vol. I, pp. xiii-xvii. J. H. Fichter, S.J., has provided a convenient popularization in *Man of Spain: Francis Suarez* (New York: Macmillan, 1940).

Very few studies that are at once penetrating and objective have been published on the philosophical thought of Suarez. Among the better, the following may be listed: E. Conze, *Der Begriff der Metaphysik bei Franciscus Suarez* (Leipzig: Felix Meiner, 1928), and M. Grabmann, "Die Disputationes metaphysicae des Franz Suarez in ihrer methodischen Eigenart and Fortwirkung," *Mittelalterliches Geistesleben*, I (München: Max Hueber, 1926), 525-60. An interesting contrast in interpretation is found in D. Fahey, "The Metaphysics of Suarez," *Irish Ecclesiastical Record*, XXIII (1924), 389-415, 485-500, if compared with P. Descoqs, S.J. "Thomisme et Suarézism," *Archives de Philosophie*, IV (1926), 434-544, and L. Teixidor, S.J., "Suarez y S. Tomas. Notas criticas," *Estudios Eclesiásticos,* a lengthy series of articles beginning in vol. XII (1933) and continuing through successive volumes.

The dearth of exhaustive treatises is partly compensated for by a number of group studies. *P. Franz Suarez, S.J., Gedenkblätter zu seinem dreihundertjahrigen Todestag* (Innsbruck, 1917), includes:

K. Six, S.J., "P. Franz Suarez als Förderer der kirchlichen Wissenschaft," pp. 1-27.

M. Grabmann, "Die Disputationes metaphysicae des Franz Suarez in ihrer methodischen Eigenart and Fortwirking," pp. 29-73. (This is the first draft of the longer and improved article cited above in *Mittelalterliches Geistesleben*).

F. Hatheyer, S.J., "Die Lehre des P. Suarez über Beschauung und Ekstase," pp. 73-122.

A. Inauer, S.J., "Suarez Widerlegung der scotistischen Körperlichkeitsform," pp. 123-46.

J. Biederlach, S.J., "Die Völkerrechtslehre des Franz Suarez," pp. 147-69.

In Italy the celebration of the tercentenary of Suarez' death issued in A. Gemelli, O.F.M. (ed.), *Scritti vari, pubblicati in occasione del terzo centenario della morte di Francesco Suarez,* (Milano, 1918). This work comprises:

A. Bernareggi, "La personalita scientifica di Francesco Suarez."

N. Monaco, S.J., "La metafisica di Suarez e la metafisica di S. Tommaso d'Aquino."

A. Masnovo, "Un problema e la sua importanza presso F. Suarez."

U. de Ercilla, S.J., "Suarez come filosofo del diritto."

A. Gemelli, "La sovranità del popolo nelle dottrine politiche di F. Suarez."

G. Semeria, "Il regicidio nella morale del Suarez."

G. B. Tragella, "La psicologia del Suarez."

S. Ritter, "Bibliografia Suareziana."

A good exposition of some phases of Suarezian philosophy is found in "A Symposium on Suarez," in *The Jesuit Educational Association, Central States Division, Proceedings of the Tenth Annual Convention* (Chicago: Loyola U. Press, 1931). This contains:

J. V. Kelly, S.J., "The Political Theory of Suarez," pp. 155-162.

G. H. Mahowald, S.J., "Suarez, De Anima," pp. 162-71.

J. F. McCormick, S.J., "Suarez on Matter and Form," pp. 172-83.

P. E. Nolan, S.J., "The Suarezian Modes," pp. 184-200.

J. G. Krost, S.J., "Suarez's Teaching on Individuation," pp. 200-211.

J. F. McCormick, S.J., "A Suarezian Bibliography," pp. 212-4.

For contributions by American scholars, we should add: J. F. McCormick, S.J., "The Significance of Suarez for a Revival of Scholasticism," in C. A. Hart (ed.), *Aspects of the New Scholastic Philosophy* (New York: Benziger, 1932); C. C. Riedl, "Suarez and the Organization of Learning," in G. Smith, S.J., (ed.), *Jesuit Thinkers of the Renaissance* (Milwaukee: Marquette U. Press, 1939); and H. Guthrie, "The Metaphysics of Francis Suarez," *Thought,* XVI (1941), 297-311, plus G. Smith's communication on p. 776 of the same volume.

The Suarezian theory of distinctions proposed in Disputation VII has never, so far as I have been able to ascertain, been made the object of explicit and extensive investigation in any published monographs.

FRANCIS SUAREZ

ON THE VARIOUS KINDS OF DISTINCTIONS

[handwritten margin note: unity: an attribute or property of being]

THE present disputation seems necessary at this point to complete our treatise on the attribute or property of being we call unity. For, since unity implies a negation of division, and is therefore opposed to multitude, which arises from division or distinction, a comprehension of all the kinds of distinction is required for a comprehension of all the kinds of unity. The reason is that the number of predicates proper to one of a pair of opposites corresponds to the number of predicates proper to the other. The investigation of this metaphysical problem is no less necessary than arduous. As Aristotle indicates in *Posterior Analytics*, Bk. II, chap. 14,[1] we grasp the essence or quiddity of any object by a process of division or distinction, since we arrive at a true definition of a thing by dividing one factor from another. Accordingly the explanation of the various degrees and kinds of distinctions is fully as difficult as the knowledge of the essences of things. In spite of this inherent difficulty we proceed to investigate the number of different kinds of distinctions, and the signs or norms by which they may be recognized.

SECTION I

WHETHER BESIDES A REAL AND A MENTAL DISTINCTION THERE IS SOME OTHER KIND OF DISTINCTION IN THINGS

1. *The existence and nature of a real distinction.* In this section *[handwritten margin note: A REAL DISTINCTION]* two propositions are assumed as certain, and a third is the object of our inquiry. First of all, it is self-evident that there is a real distinction among things. For greater clarity this is usually called a distinction between thing and thing. It consists in the fact that one thing is not another, and vice versa. As is quite obvious, many things exist of which one is not another. But we should note that frequently things are not only really distinct, but are not even united to one another, as is the case with two supposita, or with accidents which inhere in distinct supposita, and the like. It is not hard to recognize a real distinction in these, because

---

[1] *Analytica Posteriora*, II, 14, 98a 1-12. Junta I, text 85, fol. 229vb 35-53. In addition to the usual Bekker citations, reference will also be made to the Junta edition, 9 vols., Venice, 1552, except in note 12 below.

there is no vestige of real identity in them. However it sometimes happens that really distinct things are united to one another, as is clear in the case of matter and form, or quantity and substance. In such instances it is often extremely difficult to perceive a real distinction, a distinction of thing from thing; for there may be in things a distinction that is less than a real distinction of this sort. This problem will presently engage our attention. We shall also explain how one distinction may be discerned from another.

2. *Positive and negative distinctions, and their nature.* A further observation to be made about this distinction is that it is customarily divided into positive and negative. This division arises not so much from the nature of the distinction itself as from its extremes; for the distinction itself always consists formally in a negation, as was said above. The negation sometimes distinguishes between positive, real things, one of which is not the other, and then it is termed a positive distinction. This is properly the real distinction of which we have been speaking.

At times, however, there is question of such a distinction between being and non-being, or between wholly diverse non-beings, and then it is called a negative real distinction, because one of the extremes lacks the reality which the other has, if the latter is a positive and real being. Again, if each of the extremes is a privative being, such as darkness and blindness, the distinction between them is negative and real, because they are so separated and distinguished from each other that if they were positive things they would be really distinct, or at least because the foundations in which they are considered to exist in their own way are really distinct. Accordingly this negative distinction is to be understood and explained by proportion or analogy with the positive distinction. For this reason we shall omit the negative distinction, and shall treat only of the properly so-called real distinction, the positive.

3. Lastly, we should note that the present disputation has nothing to do with the question whether a real relation or only a mental relation accompanies a real distinction. For we are not here considering distinction inasmuch as it is capable of inducing formal relationship; we are concerned solely with the foundation on which such relationship may be based. Indeed, a real relation is not, formally speaking, necessary for a real distinction. God is really distinct from an angel, but has no real relation to the angel. If the objection is made that at least the angel has a real relation to God, the answer is forthcoming that whatever be the truth in this point, the angel is apprehended to be a thing distinct from God prior to any such relationship. The relationship, if there is any, results from the distinction. Again, in God the three Persons are really distinct, although the distinction among them is not a special

[17]

relation. Consequently the question of relation is to be omitted as not pertinent to the present inquiry.

4. *The existence and nature of a mental distinction.* In the second place, it is certain that besides real distinctions there are mental distinctions. This sort of distinction does not formally and actually intervene between the things designated as distinct, as they exist in themselves, but only as they exist in our ideas, from which they receive some denomination. Thus we distinguish one attribute from another in God, or the relation of identity from its term, as when we say that Peter is the same as himself. Mental distinctions are usually considered to be of two kinds. One, which has no foundation in reality, is called a distinction of the reasoning reason *(distinctio rationis ratiocinantis)*, because it arises exclusively from the reflection and activity of the intellect. The other, which has a foundation in reality, is called by many a distinction of the reasoned reason *(distinctio rationis ratiocinatae)*, although this is a highly improper term and can be equivocal. For this type of mental distinction can be understood as pre-existing in reality, prior to the discriminating operation of the mind, so as to be thought of as imposing itself, as it were, on the intellect, and to require the intellect only to recognize it, but not to constitute it. In this acceptation of the term the distinction would be called mental rather than real only because it is not so great, and in itself is not so evident, as a real distinction, and hence would need attentive inspection by the mind to discern it.

With the meaning of the term thus explained according to its etymology, I wish to point out that such a distinction is not the true mental distinction we are dealing with at present, but coincides with a distinction from the nature of the case, of which we shall treat in due course. In another sense, however, there can be question of a distinction of the reasoned reason: a distinction of the reason, because actually and formally it is not found in reality, but has its origin in the mind; a distinction of the reasoned reason, because it arises not entirely from the sheer operation of the intellect, but from the occasion offered by the thing itself on which the mind is reflecting. Hence the foundation that is held to exist in nature for this distinction is not a true and actual distinction between the things regarded as distinct; for then not the foundation of the distinction but the distinction itself would precede mental operation. Rather the foundation must be either the eminence **of the object** which the mind thus distinguishes (with a distinction that many call virtual), or at any rate it must be some reference to other things which are truly distinct in the real order, and with respect to which such a distinction is excogitated or conceived.

[18]

5. These two kinds of mental distinction, though variously explained by different authors, may conveniently be described as follows. The distinction of the reasoning reason is ordered to one and the same adequate or simple concept of an object solely through a mental repetition or comparison of the object. Thus Peter is distinguished from himself either according to subject and predicate, when he is predicated of himself, or according to the term and subject of a relation, when he is said to be the same as himself. In these and like mental distinctions the concept of Peter remains unchanged and is adequate, and there is made only a certain repetition and comparison of it.

The other kind of mental distinction arises from inadequate concepts of one and the same thing. Although the same object is apprehended in each concept, the whole reality contained in the object is not adequately represented, nor is its entire essence and objective notion exhausted, by either of them. This occurs frequently when we conceive an object in terms of its bearing on different things, or when we represent it in the way we conceive these different things. Hence such a distinction invariably has a foundation in fact, even though formally it will be said to spring from inadequate concepts of the same thing. Thus in God we distinguish His justice from His mercy, because we do not conceive the sublimely simple virtue of God as it is in itself and according to the full range of its energy. We partition it into concepts in line with the various effects of which that eminent virtue is the principle, or by analogy with various virtues which we find distinct in man, but which in an ineffably eminent manner are found united in the absolutely simple virtue of God.

6. These considerations enable us to understand, first, that a mental distinction is not so termed because it intervenes between entities of the mind *(entia rationis)*, although many have erroneously held this, as we shall see later. As is clear from the instances cited, things said to be thus distinct are real entities, or rather a single real entity conceived according to various aspects. The same is evident from the fact that reason does not produce the entities it thus distinguishes, but merely conceives things which are not distinct as though they were distinct. Hence it is not the objects distinguished but only the distinction itself that results from the reasoning.

Nevertheless the mind does not err in thus distinguishing, because it does not assert that things conceived in this manner are distinct in fact, but simply and without composition — that is, without affirmation or denial — conceives them as distinct through precisive abstraction whereby it effects, as it were, this type of distinction. If later it predicates such reflection or composition of objects so conceived, it does not affirm simply, but only in a qualified manner, that is, according to the viewpoint of the mind, that they are distinct. Further, although this distinction does not require extremes that are in themselves entities of the mind, it always supposes in them a certain denomination received from the mind, such as the denomination of subject or predicate, or at least supposes that the extremes are conceived partially and inadequately.

Accordingly, although this distinction does not require extremes that are in every sense entities of the mind, it can be imagined or thought of as existing between such entities; for once an entity of the mind has been conceived, it can be compared with itself, and so can be mentally distinguished. Indeed even the relation of species, for example, which in itself is a single entity of the mind adequately comprehending all its individuals, can be precisely conceived as referring to one or the other individual, and hence can be mentally distinguished. Therefore, although the mental distinction does not require entities of the mind as its extremes, and does not receive its designation from such entities, it can be extended to them or intervene between them.

7. Extrinsic and intrinsic mental distinctions. Such considerations lead to the realization that there is a twofold mental distinction. First, there is the intrinsic mental distinction, which in itself is not a true distinction but is merely conceived as such or produced by the mind. This is properly the mental distinction of which we are speaking. In a second sense there can be question of a distinction termed mental as it were extrinsically, that is, from the extremes between which it is apprehended to exist; the distinction is called mental because it intervenes between extremes that are altogether entities of the mind. This is not always a mental distinction in the first sense, but only when it has to do with one and the same entity of the mind, as has been explained.

Of course a distinction can be made between two entities of the mind. This is not a real distinction, since the entities are not real. On the other hand it is not an intrinsic mental distinction in the proper sense, because such as they are these extremes are of themselves truly distinct, and not merely through intellectual fiction. Since a distinction is a negation, it can be verified even of entities of the mind, and so it is rather a quasi-real distinction, as was said above concerning the distinction between darkness and blindness. A similar distinction is apprehended between the relations of two sets of species to their individuals, for example, such as is conceived in human nature with respect to its individuals, and in equine nature with respect to its individuals. These two relations are compared with each other in such a way that if they were real entities they would be really distinct; for they have foundations and terms that are really distinct.

8. The origin of mental distinctions. Lastly, as will be understood from what has been established, the properly so-called and intrinsic mental distinction of which we are speaking does not exist strictly by itself, but only dependently on the mind that conceives things in an imperfect, abstractive, and confused manner, or inadequately. Since this distinction is not found in nature nor in the object known, it consists solely in a certain denomination issuing from concepts of the mind, and hence requires a distinction at least in the concepts themselves and in the denomination derived from them. However, since the object which is the basis of the distinction is absolutely a unit, the distinction between the concepts has its origin solely in the imperfection of the concepts themselves. For this reason the divine intellect never makes a mental distinction in any proper sense, although it perfectly understands the distinction originating in the finite intellect that conceives imperfectly.

The Heart of the Question. Various Opinions

9. With these preliminary matters disposed of, we come to the central problem: whether, in addition to these two kinds of distinctions a third kind is to be admitted, which would occupy as it were a middle position between the other two.

Many deny that any such intermediate distinction can be thought of or understood. This is the opinion of Durandus, *In I Sent.*, d. 2, q. 2; Ockham, *In I Sent.*, q. 3; Hervaeus, *Quodl.* III, q. 3; John of Ghent, *Metaph.*, VI, q. 10; Soncinas, *Quaestiones metaphysicales*, VII, q. 36. Similar views are held by Cajetan, *In I Part.*, q. 54, a. 2; and Soto, *Univer.*, q. 3, and *Capit. de Prop.*, q. 2. But in these authors we must be on the watch for equivocation, and ascertain whether they disagree with us in doctrine or only in terminology. To be sure, we can think of no distinction between positive, real extremes that would not necessarily pre-exist in actuality prior to all intellectual operation — unless, of course, the distinction is constituted by the mind. Since, moreover, whatever exists in this way is real inasmuch as it exists in nature, any distinction which is not mental can be termed real in this sense. Therefore it seems altogether clear that there can be no middle ground between a real and a mental distinction.

Nevertheless, this being presupposed, there still remains the question whether every distinction between things prior to all mental activity is actually and formally, and not merely fundamentally and virtually, of the same nature on the ground that it intervenes between distinct things, or whether there may be a major and a minor distinction in things themselves, so that the major distinction, namely that between thing and thing, would pre-empt the name of real distinction, and the minor would be called an intermediate distinction or would be designated by other terms to be explained later.

[21]

Consequently, if the authors enumerated deny the intermediate distinction between real and mental in the first sense alone, they differ merely in terminology from those who admit it. Indeed, some inconsistency is noted in certain authors who at times deny the intermediate distinction, at times make use of it. This is the case particularly with Soto, as appears from an examination of the passages cited, as well as his chapter on *Relation*, and elsewhere. However, if they deny the intermediate distinction in the second sense, there will be dissension mainly in doctrine.

10. With the intermediate distinction understood in this latter sense, at first sight the opinion which denies it, seems to commend itself. There are not more kinds of distinctions than there are kinds of beings, for unity and multiplicity are attendant on being, and it is through distinction that multiplicity has its origin. But there are no classes of being besides real and mental entities, as we gather from Aristotle, *Metaphysics*, Bk. V. text. 14,[2] and Bk. VI, text. 6.[3] For, since these two imply a direct contradiction, no medium between them can be excogitated.

Secondly, whatever beings exist in the actual order prior to mental activity are either really identified or are really diverse, as otherwise there would be a middle ground between "the same" and "other", which is contrary to Aristotle, *Metaphysics*, Bk. IV, text. 4,[4] and text. 5,[5] where he states that sameness and diversity adequately divide being, just as one and many do; and in Bk. X, text. 11,[6] he remarks that any given being as compared with another is either the same as it or other than it. The reason is that these are opposed by immediate contradiction. Hence just as sameness and diversity in general, so a definite and real sameness and diversity are proper to each being with reference to another.

Accordingly all objects which we conceive as two entities are either really the same or are really other. If they are really other they are really distinct. If they are really the same they cannot be distinct in the real order antecedently to intellectual advertence, as it is impossible for a thing to be simultaneously the same and other in the real order.

11. If it should be maintained that there is no repugnance in having sameness in the common notion of being along with diversity in the notion of such or such being, for example of quality or relation, action or passion, I take my stand against this position.

In the third place, then, if an inferior predicate is multiplied, the corresponding superior predicate must likewise be multiplied; but any determinate aspects of beings are inferior to being as such; therefore in

[2] *Metaphysica*, V, 7, 1017a 22-b 9. Junta VIII, fol. 55 ra 48-b 22.
[3] *Ibid.*, VI, 4 (1027a 19-26). Junta VIII, fol. 70 vb 25-34.
[4] *Ibid.*, IV, 2, 1004a1-b7 Junta VIII, fol. 30 rb. 64-va 50.
[5] *Ibid.*, IV, 2, 1004b7-26. Junta VII, fol. 33rb 14-56.
[6] *Ibid.*, X, 3, 1054b, 14-15. Junta VIII, fol. 121 vb 10-11.

the real order there can be no multiplication under determinate aspects of beings, for instance under the aspect of quality or relation, whiteness or similarity, unless there is multiplication under the general notion of being. Therefore, if there is plurality under these determinate aspects, there is also a plurality of beings; and hence there can be no distinction among such aspects in the real order unless these are really distinct.

The initial proposition in this line of reasoning seems self-evident in the light of what was established above concerning universals.[7] For the same universal or common attribute which is numerically one and the same in the real order cannot be contracted or determined by opposing differences or modes. This is why we asserted[8] that unity under some common aspect is not true and real unity in fact, but is only a likeness observed in the thing and a unity imparted by the mind. Therefore if certain determinate aspects of being are multiplied in the real order, it follows that along with them the very notion of being must be multiplied in the real order. Any two such aspects, inasmuch as they are by nature distinct, imply opposite or mutually exclusive modes or differences whereby they are distinguished from each other. Hence they cannot possess true and real identity or numerical unity in the order of being, seeing that an entity, while it remains numerically the same, cannot be modified and determined by opposing differences.

To confirm this conclusion we need only reflect that otherwise there could be a single accident in a thing and nevertheless two qualities, and quality together with quantity; and in the same way one substance could be two bodies; or a single animal could be simultaneously a horse and a lion, and so on. If open contradiction is perceived in these instances, the same will be true of all things that are really distinct according to their proper notions, with respect to any superior whatsoever, including being itself. For being itself is comprised in all inferior aspects no less essentially than are the intermediate predicates. And there is the further reason that the opposing and distinguishing differences involve the same repugnance with regard to the same individual, under whatever superior or inferior aspect it may be regarded.

12. In the fourth place, this same position may be explained in yet another way. Whatever exists in reality has its own real essence. Therefore things that are really distinct have in reality distinct essences either numerically, if they are only numerically distinct, or specifically or generically, if they are assumed to be essentially distinct. Consequently they have in reality distinct entities, which is what is meant by a real distinction.

This conclusion is clear for two reasons. First, the entity of a thing is nothing but its real essence as it exists outside its causes; but if the

[7] Cf. Disp. VI, sect. 1, no. 11.
[8] Ibid., sect. 5, no. 1 f.

essences are distinct, they exist really outside their causes; therefore they will be distinct entities. Secondly, if we have here two real essences, each of them is the essence of some real being, for being and essence are adequately compared as abstract and concrete; but one and the same being can have no more than one essence; therefore, if there are two real essences, there are two real beings.

This latter minor seems self-evident, since a thing has unity chiefly from its essence, and nothing can be more invariable, fixed, and certain in a thing than its essence. Again, if a thing is constituted by one essence, it has in consequence its ultimate differentia and species, and hence is no longer determinable. Accordingly one and the same thing cannot be actuated, determined, or constituted by the differentia of another species. Therefore it cannot have any other essence, and so if there is another distinct essence it constitutes another thing.

13. *The teaching of Scotus in his formal distinction.* A second opinion is this: there is in things prior to intellectual activity a certain actual distinction, which accordingly is greater than a mental distinction, but still is not so great as the real distinction between thing and thing. This theory is commonly attributed to Scotus, *In I Sent.,* d. 2, q. 7, last paragraph; dist. 5, q. 1; dist. 8, q. 4; *In II Sent.,* dist. 3, q. 1. The doctrine is also brought out in innumerable other texts wherein Scotus discourses on the distinction between God's attributes, or the distinction between universals, and similar matters. In such passages, however, Scotus does not explain with sufficient clarity whether this distinction, which he himself calls formal, is actual in the real order or merely fundamental or virtual. Sometimes he refers to it as virtual, and so there are various interpretations among his followers.

Some think that for Scotus himself the formal distinction is no other than the distinction of the reasoned reason, in the sense and manner explained by us. They say that it is called formal because various definitions or formal aspects are conceived in it; and they say further that it is called a distinction from the nature of the case because it has a foundation in things themselves and is virtually in them, although actually it does not precede mental operation. According to this interpretation Scotus does not favor the second opinion; nor does there seem to be any doubt that in some passages this is the mind of Scotus, especially when he is treating of the divine attributes.

Other disciples of Scotus understand him to speak of a true and actual distinction which is verified in reality antecedently to the advertence of the mind, and they think that it is found not only among creatures, but also in God, at least between the divine relations and essence. In this matter Durandus holds the same opinion, *In I Sent.,* dist. 1, part. 2; d. 5.

q. 2, ad 4; and at greater length in d. 33, q. 1. A number of others defend this view, but it would take too long to recount their explanations. In favor of this same opinion many could be cited who admit a distinction from the nature of the case, but not a real distinction, between various things, for example between existence and essence, nature and suppositum, quantity and substance, relation and its foundation, and the like, as we shall see later when treating of these topics.[9]

14. *Whether the Scotist distinction is according to the mind of Aristotle.* This view is often attributed to Aristotle, for the reason that in his *Physics*, Bk. III,[10] he teaches that the same motion is at once action and passion under diverse formalities. And in Bk. IV[11] he similarly distinguishes time from motion, although he indicates that the former is not a distinct thing from the latter. Again, in his work *On Generation and Corruption*, Bk. I,[12] he seems to establish a like distinction between nutrition and growth, stating that they are the same in subject, that is, in their entity, but are distinct in their actual being, that is, in the formal being proper to each. And lastly in the *Categories*[13] he places the same quality, for instance heat, under different species, which is unintelligible unless two species can be really identical while they are formally distinct.

But these testimonies are not very cogent, because in the first two examples, as also in the last, a mental distinction through inadequate concepts suffices; this point we shall develop at greater length when we come to treat of accidents and predicaments.[14] In the second example, moreover, the interpretation does violence to the words of Aristotle, for whom "to be the same in subject" means simply, as the terms themselves imply, to be united in the same subject or suppositum, whereas distinction according to being means rather to be distinct in entity or form. Similarly in *Physics*, Bk. I, text. 21,[15] Aristotle says that to be white and to be musical may be the same in reality, but are distinct according to reason. Here his use of these terms is highly equivocal, as by reason he means essence or definition, and by reality he means the subject or suppositum in which these qualities inhere. In this sense his statement can or indeed ought to be interpreted when he says that nutrition and growth are the same in subject, but are distinct according to their being,

---

[9] On the distinction between essence and existence, see Disp. XXXI, sect. 1 and 6; on the distinction between nature and suppositum, Disp. XXXIV, sect 2; on the distinction between quantity and substance, Disp. XL, sect. 2; on the distinction between relation and its foundation, Disp. XLVII, sect. 2 and 7.

[10] *Physica*, III, 3. 202a 36-b. 22. Junta IV, text 19-22. fol. 44 ra 50-vb 69.

[11] *Ibid.*, IV, 10-12, (218b 10-221a 30, *passim*). Junta IV, text 95-117, fol. 81 vb 42-88 rb 45.

[12] *De generatione et corruptione*, I, 5 (322a 20-26). Junta (Venice, 1560), V, text 41, fol. 287 b 15-20

[13] *Categoriae*, 8 (8b 36; 9a 30). Junta I, fol. 21 va 55; vb. 43.

[14] Cf. Disp. XXXIX; esp. sect. 2, no. 22.

[15] *Physica*, I, 2, 185b 32-34. Junta IV, fol. 8 ra 50-53.

especially if nutrition here means change as terminating in substance, and growth means change as terminating in quantity. But if both are taken as terminating in quantity, they can be distinguished only by reason or by their relation to each other, inasmuch as the quantity acquired is greater than or equal to the quantity lost. But we shall deal with this matter on another occasion.[16]

From these and similar texts of Aristotle, then, no solid argument for this opinion can be derived. And I judge the same of St. Thomas and other ancient authors, who practically always employ the terms "real distinction" and "mental distinction" in the first sense as explained above, and do not treat explicitly the question which at present concerns us.

15. This theory is based mainly on a suasive argument drawn from reason. Whatever extends beyond the essential definition of a thing is in some sense really distinct from it; but many elements extend beyond the essence of a thing without being themselves things distinct from the thing in question; therefore there is a distinction in the real order that is less than a real distinction. In other words: whatever aspects are distinct by definition and objective concept, are distinct by the nature of the case and prior to intellectual consideration; but many aspects are thus distinct, although they are not distinct as thing from thing; therefore. These and like arguments are advanced by Scotists, since this is about the way Scotus himself seems to propose his formal distinction. However, if we closely examine such arguments, we find either that the question is begged or that the formal distinction is substituted for the distinction of the reasoned reason through inadequate concepts; only virtually or fundamentally can this distinction be said to be based on the nature of the case.

What we are contending may be demonstrated, or rather explained, as follows. We do not always define the essence of a thing as it is in itself, but as we conceive it. Thus we define the essence of man as though it were general, although in fact it is singular. Hence if we are speaking of essence in this fashion, it is false that whatever extends beyond essence is actually distinct in the real order from what is essential, as is clear from what was said above[17] on individuation, specific nature, and other universals, particularly genus and differentia, of which the authors mentioned seem mostly to speak. This is the way, it seems, they understand essence in the first argument. But if they are speaking of essence as it is in reality, this is nothing else than the very entity of the thing, and hence if they assume that there is some element in a thing

[16] See Disp. XL, sect. 3, nos. 11-13; Disp. XLI, sect. 5, nos. 10-14.
[17] Disp. V, sect. 2; Disp. VI, sect. 2 and 9.

[26]

which is distinct from the essence, but which is not a distinct thing, they suppose precisely what ought to be proved. The second argument is weaker still. The major is not universally true, since many things are distinguished in objective concepts according to our point of view, although they are only mentally distinct through inadequate concepts, as is clear from what we have written of the notion of being, of the individual, of species and the other universals.[18] All these can be distinguished in definition by a mere mental distinction, whenever a definition does not adequately represent a thing as it is in itself, but as it is exhibited in a concept of ours.

Solution of the Question

16. Notwithstanding, I think it is true without qualification that there is among created things a certain actual distinction which is found in nature prior to any activity of the mind, and that such distinction is not so great as the distinction between two altogether separate things or entities. This distinction, to be sure, could be designated by the general term "real", inasmuch as it is truly verified in reality, and is not merely an extrinsic denomination issuing from the intellect. However, to differentiate it from the other, namely the major real distinction, we can call it either a "distinction from the nature of the case," thus applying to this imperfect distinction a term that is in common use, or more properly a "modal distinction." For, as I shall explain, this distinction is invariably found to intervene between a thing and its mode.

The term "formal distinction" is not much to my liking, as it is excessively equivocal. It is frequently applied to things really distinct, inasmuch as they are essentially distinct if they differ specifically; such objects have different formal unities, and hence differ formally. Even individuals of the same species may be said to be formally distinct, inasmuch as their individual formal unities are distinct, as we said above.[19] Indeed, even in the Trinity paternity and filiation, which are really, though not essentially or numerically distinct, can be said to be formally distinct in the objective notions of their relations — a kind of distinction not found outside this mystery.

Thus a formal distinction is of wider extension, and can be greater than the distinction from the nature of the case, of which we are speaking. From another point of view it can be a lesser distinction, and this is the more common acceptation, for it is frequently applied to formalities as conceived in a state of precision by our minds. In this latter sense the distinction does not exceed the level of a mental distinction.

---

[18] See Disp. II, and the references cited in the preceding note.
[19] Disp. V, sect. 4 and 6.

17. Let me come to the explanation and proof of my assertion. I assume that in created things, besides their entities which are, as it were, substantial and (if I may use the term) radical, there are apprehended certain real modes that are something positive and of themselves modify the very entities by conferring on them something that is over and above the complete essence as individual and as existing in nature. This is established by induction. Thus in quantity, for example, which inheres in a substance, two aspects may be considered: one is the entity of quantity itself, the other is the union or actual inherence of this quantity in the substance.

The first we call simply the thing or being of quantity, comprising whatever pertains to the essence of the individual quantity as it is found in nature, and remains and is preserved even if quantity is separated from its subject. It is impossible to preserve this particular numerical quantity without including the essence of quantity along with its intrinsic individuation and actual existence. With this existence we shall deal later,[20] but the rest of what I have said results from what has gone before.[21]

The second aspect, inherence, we call a mode of quantity, but not in the general sense in which every quality may be termed a mode of substance, as St. Thomas says in the *Summa*, Ia-IIae, q. 49, a. 2. Nor is the term "mode" used in the wide sense in which every contracting or determining principle is called the mode of the being thus contracted. In this sense "rational" can be called the mode of "animal"; and the term is used especially with reference to those modes whereby being or accident is determined to the highest genera. Lastly, the term is not taken in the general meaning in which every determination or limitation affixed to a finite thing according to its measure is called a mode, as St. Thomas notes in the same passage, commenting on the words of St. Augustine, *De Genesi ad litteram*, Bk. IV, chap. 3:[22] "Mode is that which a measure determines." Speaking of mode in this sense Augustine says in *De natura boni*, chap. 3,[23] that three factors are necessary for the goodness of any created thing; two of these are species and order, and the third is mode, that is, a due commensuration to its principles, as St. Thomas explains in Ia, q. 5, [a. 5], and Ia-IIae, q. 85, a. 4, and frequently elsewhere. But leaving aside this general meaning of mode and applying the notion to the present case, the inherence of quantity is called its mode because it is something affecting quantity and, as it were, ultimately determining its state and manner of existing, without adding to it a proper new entity, but merely modifying a pre-existing entity.

---

20 Disp. XXXI, sect. 1, no. 13; and sections 4, 5, and 6.
21 Disp. V, sect. 7; sect. 9, no. 20 f.
22 *PL*, XXXIV, 229.
23 *PL*, XLII, 553.

18. That inherence does not add a proper new entity can scarcely be doubted. If it were an altogether new entity, it could not be the actual union between quantity and its subject, but would require some medium for union with subject and quantity, just as quantity itself requires an inherence whereby it is united to its subject. If, then, the inherence does not need a further union or inherence by which it may be united or may inhere, the reason is that the inherence does not add a real entity which inheres and is united, but is merely a certain mode that of itself is the reason for union and inherence. Another indication of this is that the inherence has a mode of being such that it cannot exist unless it is actually joined to the form of which it is the inherence, and that this particular inherence can modify or rather unite only this particular form to which it is, so to speak, affixed. Such a mode of affecting is never found in those forms or things which have proper entities of themselves.

What has been said of the inherence of quantity holds also for quality, for the union of substantial form with matter, for subsistence or personality with respect to nature, for presence and local motion, and for all action or dependence with respect to its terminus. But this is not the place to discuss all these questions; they will all come up in the course of the present work.[24] I will explain briefly only the last instance, as it seems to be the easiest. Thus light, for example, depends on the sun; and this dependence is something other than light or the sun. We can conceive that light and the sun would remain, without light depending on the sun, if God were to refuse to concur with the sun for the production or conservation of light, and would keep both in being by His own power alone. But we cannot conceive the dependence of light on the sun to be an entity wholly distinct from the light itself, for two reasons. First, this dependence is, so to speak, the channel through which the cause flows into its effect or terminus, and so the dependence cannot be something entirely distinct from the effect. Secondly, otherwise this entity, the dependence, would be separable from the other entity, namely the light, at least as regards God's absolute power; but this is quite unintelligible. Consequently the dependence is a certain mode of light itself, a mode which some, perhaps, would call a relation. However it is not a predicamental relation, but implies a transcendental relation or ordination, as will be explained more fully below.[25] Accordingly there are in created entities certain modes affecting these entities, and their nature seems to consist in this, that they do not of themselves suffice to

---

24 Cf. Disp. XLII, sect. 1; Disp. XIII, sect. 9, no. 11 f., and Disp. XV, sect. 6, nos. 6-10; Disp. XXXIV, sect. 2 and 4; Disp. XLIX, sect. 2, nos. 4-6; Disp. LI, sect 1; Disp. XLVIII, sect. 2.
25 Disp. XLVII, sect. 4, esp. no. 15.

Modes can't exist w/out an entity

constitute being or entity in the real order of things, but are intrinsically directed to the actual modification of some entity without which they are quite incapable of existing.

19. *Why modes are only modally distinct from things.* A posteriori the reason for postulating these modes is based on induction. A priori the reason seems to be that, since creatures are imperfect, and hence either dependent or composite or limited or mutable according to various states of presence, union, and termination, they require these modes by which all those characteristics may be brought to realization. It is not always necessary, or even readily intelligible, that these characteristics be always produced by entities which are wholly distinct; nor can they be brought about by what is absolutely nothing. Therefore at least a real mode is required. What the number of these modes is, and under which predicament they are to be classified directly or reductively, I shall explain later when dealing with the divisions of predicaments.[26]

Further, Durandus seems to be aware of such modes, *In I Sent.,* d. 30, q. 2, no. 15, where he says that the being-in or inherence of accidents is an aspect which is analogously called a thing or being, since it is not a thing but a mode of being, and is not an entity having mode, but is merely a mode of entity; and in no. 16 he says the same of dependence, and of everything that is a mere mode of being. Astudillo, in *De generatione,* I, q. 5, ad 1, speaks of inherence in the same fashion. And in particular when treating of subsistence, many authors explain the matter in such a way, as for example Giles of Rome, *De compositione angelorum,* q. 5. Finally Fonseca, in his commentary on Aristotle's *Metaphysics,* Bk. V, chap. 6, q. 6, sect. 2, expressly mentions these modes, although he divides them into three classes.

First, (says Fonseca), there are some modes which of themselves are entities distinct from others, as whiteness and sweetness. In this class he also places figure, though wrongly, for figure belongs to the third class, since it modifies quantity as a mode, not as a thing entirely distinct from quantity. Secondly, there are modes which not only are not distinct entities but are in no way really distinct from the things they are said to modify, but are only mentally distinct, as for example the modes whereby being is contracted to its inferiors. But we pass over these two classes of modes; the latter are not modes except by intellectual perception, and the former are things or forms possessing proper entities in their own right. In the third class Fonseca places those modes which we call real modes in the proper and technical sense of the term. His view of these is that which we have proposed, although he suggests some illustrations that do not seem sound to us. Such is the example of the

---

[26] Disp XXXII, sect. 1.

[30]

existence of created things, and the mode whereby a thing is designated necessary or contingent, or a being is termed complete or incomplete.

This latter instance surely can be equivocal. If these predicates are applied to a whole and its integral parts, it is true that there is a certain mode pertaining to quantity. Thus a portion of water, if self-contained and separated from other portions of water, is called a complete or total being; but if it is continuous with other portions of water it is called a partial or incomplete being; and so we have a mode that consists solely in diverse union or termination. If, however, these predicates are applied to being as it is in itself they pertain rather to the intrinsic and essential modes of being, whether being is said to be logically incomplete, such as specific difference, or physically and really incomplete, such as the rational soul, which is called incomplete being not by reason of anything added to its essence, but because of its own essence. Hence this mode is only mentally distinct from it. The same appears to me to be the case with the mode of necessary or contingent being, if these predicates are considered in the absolute sense of being; but if they are considered from the viewpoint of their effects they are extrinsic denominations, as we shall point out below.[27] As for existence, there is spirited controversy, as we shall show in a later disputation.[28]

But whatever is to be thought of the examples he adduces, Fonseca states most truly that this sort of mode is not properly a thing or an entity, except in the widest and most general sense of the term "being", as designating whatever is not nothing. But if we understand by entity that which of itself and in itself is something, in the sense that it does not intrinsically and essentially require to be always attached to something else, but is either incapable of union with another thing or at least cannot be united except through the mediation of another mode that is naturally distinct from it, a mode is not, properly speaking, a thing or entity. Its imperfection is clearly brought out by the fact that it must invariably be affixed to something else to which it is per se and directly joined without the medium of another mode, as, for instance, sitting is joined to the sitter, union to the things united, and so of other cases of which there will be frequent mention in the following pages. *[margin: on modes (i.e. the sitting sitter)]*

20. In the light of the foregoing both the meaning and the proof of our position are easily understood. For this mode, in the sense explained, is by the nature of the case actually distinct from the thing it modifies, as all acknowledge. Many go so far as to call this a real distinction, because it is found in things themselves, as will appear more clearly in the doctrine to be presented in the next section. Yet this mode is not properly distinct from the subject it modifies, as thing from thing.

[27] Disp. XIX, sect. 10.
[28] Disp. XXXI, sections 1, 4, 5, 6, 7.

Therefore it is distinct with a lesser distinction, which is most aptly called a modal distinction.

The minor premise is true, first, because a mode, considered precisely in itself, is not properly a thing or entity, as has been sufficiently explained; hence it is not properly distinct as thing from thing. Secondly, this mode so necessarily includes conjunction with the thing of which it is a mode that it is unable by any power whatsoever to exist apart from that thing. This is a sign that such conjunction is a certain mode of identity. Accordingly there is a lesser distinction between this mode and its subject than there is between two things. All this will receive further confirmation in the following section, wherein we shall set forth the signs of these distinctions, and consequently the differences by which they are distinguished from one another.

21. *Besides modal, real, and mental distinctions, no further distinction is possible.* I submit, finally, that besides real, modal, and mental distinctions there is no other which is not common to these, or is not comprised in them. I am led to make this statement because of some authors who add a formal distinction, such as intervenes between man and animal; and this they divide into mutual distinction, as between animal and rational, and non-mutual distinction, as between animal and man. Some also propose an essential distinction, as between man and horse, and a potential distinction, as between the parts of a continuum. Similar distinctions are multiplied, but it seems to me without necessity.

The adequateness of the division given is easily gathered from what has been established. If the extremes of a distinction are not actually distinct at all in the real order, we invariably have a mental distinction. It may be called by other names, but a different name would suit it only by extrinsic denomination, inasmuch as the same thing is the object of, or is subordinated to, different conceptions. In this type of distinction, however, various degrees are discernible, as I have pointed out,[29] and so when the distinction has a foundation in reality, and is the result of several inadequate concepts, it can be called a formal distinction, or at times even an essential distinction, according to mental perception. A number of types is possible within this very class, inasmuch as the extremes can be compared according to various aspects, namely as determinate and indeterminate, for example being and substance; or as whole and part, for example differentia and species; or as two co-parts, for example animal and rational. Likewise this distinction can be understood as intervening between that which comprises and the thing comprised, or between extremes neither one of which logically includes the other. In this sense and no other such a distinction can be called

---

[29] See nos. 4-6.

mutual or non-mutual, reciprocal or non-reciprocal. In any case, all of these fall under the general classification of mental distinction.

But if the extremes of a distinction are actually distinct in the real order, either each is a true thing having its own simple or composite entity, or one extreme is a thing and the other is a mode of that thing. In the former alternative we have a real distinction, in the latter a modal distinction. No other relation between such extremes is intelligible; nor can any other medium between them be thought of. For they imply an immediate opposition, as it were of contradiction, between themselves. Therefore no other kind of distinction is possible beyond those listed.

22. *Various types of real distinction.* However in the real distinction itself, that is, the distinction between several things, we can consider various types or various relations. First, we can conceive that things thus distinct may be not only really distinct, but dissimilar in their intrinsic and essential entity. In this case they are said to be not only really but essentially distinct; and according as such dissimilarity is greater or less the objects are said to be distinct in their ultimate species, or in their subordinate species, or even in genus or predicament. Hence essential distinction is either common to real, modal, and mental distinctions; or, if taken in its most proper sense, it is included in the class of real distinction, although it is not convertible with the latter. It connotes the idea of dissimilarity rather than of distinction.

All this supposes that the term "essential distinction" is employed in the strict sense. For if there is question of a distinction of essences, such as obtains even between individuals, as we said above,[30] this does not properly add anything but points out things between which there is a distinction; thus a distinction between persons is called a personal distinction. Again, things so distinct can at times be united to each other, at times to a single third. In the former way matter and form are united, and likewise integral continuous parts, to omit other unions that are more extrinsic and accidental. Accordingly, just as matter and form, though united, maintain a real distinction from each other, so too continuous parts, though united, are really distinct not only according to designation, as some say, but also according to the partial entity of each.

23. *Potential distinction truly real.* We must note that matter and form are of themselves incomplete and partial beings, whether they are united or whether they are assumed to exist separately. Hence they are always regarded as distinct in the same manner. But integral parts do not have the character of part or of incomplete being unless they are united; as soon as they are separated, each one begins to be a complete and whole entity, because it is not of itself ordained to the composition

---

[30] See no. 16.

of another thing. Thus when they are separated they are thought of as being distinct in a different way (but more according to denomination or the way they are distinguished than in reality) than when they are united. For in the separated state they are distinguished as complete beings, but when united they are distinguished as incomplete beings. Accordingly, when such parts are united, they are sometimes said to be actually distinct as parts, but potentially as beings, that is, as units of a sort, because they are in potency to become such units.

This is verified mainly in homogeneous parts of a continuum; for in heterogeneous parts, although in fact the case is practically the same, there is some difference in the type of distinction, since there is a greater dissimilarity among the parts, and so seemingly a greater distinction, even while they are still in the whole. And when such parts are separated, if they do not change their substantial form but keep the same form they had in the whole, as happens when plants have been divided or animals dismembered, they are still considered incomplete and partial beings, because of themselves they are always, as it were, ordained to the composition of something else.

From this discussion it is easy to perceive that this distinction, which by some is called potential, is a real distinction. For, since a distinction is a negation, it can deny two things: first, that this is that; and this is actually true of parts that are actually united, because one is not the other. This is the negation which of itself is chiefly requisite and sufficient for a distinction. Secondly, it can deny that this is united to that, which is the same as saying that this is not that, inasmuch as it is a complete and integral being distinct from that. This is not verified in parts that are actually united, but only in those that are in potency for union. From this latter point of view the distinction can be termed potential; nevertheless as such it does not yet exist, and so it should not be enumerated among distinctions as if it were distinct from the others.

Hence it is clear a fortiori that some authors are quite unjustified in calling the distinction between the parts of a continuum a mental distinction with foundation in fact, on the ground that such parts are not distinct in actuality, but only in designation and potency. This is not so, because here we have not merely a foundation for a distinction, but a true distinction, in the proper usage of the term, not indeed as implying separation or disunion, but as involving a difference between total and partial entity. Otherwise matter and form, when united, should not be said to be distinct in act, but only in potency, for surely the union between matter and form is not less than the union between the parts of a continuum. We could speak of a mental separation between such parts, since it is only by the discriminatory power of the mind that they can be regarded as disjoined and as units of a sort; but the distinction of the parts is actual and real. For these parts, even when they compose a whole, have a certain reality, since, as Aristotle remarks in the *Physics*, Bk. I, chap. 2,[31] a substance is not composed except of substances; so, too, a complete being is not composed except of beings that are at least partial. Therefore such beings remain distinct, though united. Indeed, unless they remained distinct they could not enter into composition, since composition results only from distinct elements.

24. *The distinction between that which comprises and the thing comprised is a real distinction.* This gives rise to a further type of distinction, which can be perceived in any whole with respect to its several parts. The whole and the parts are not entirely the same, as is self-evident; but neither are they distinct as two parts between themselves, since in the latter case neither includes the other, whereas the whole embraces both parts within its entity. Consequently the whole and the parts are said to be distinct as that which comprises and thing comprised. This distinction is real, because the whole includes something which a part does not. Accordingly this type of distinction, between that which comprises and the thing comprised, is in its own way discoverable in real, modal, and mental distinctions. For in each of these orders that which has the function of a whole can be compared with that which has the function of a part. But wherever this distinction occurs it remains within the realm of real, modal, or mental distinction, because what includes one extreme in addition to another is really, modally, or mentally distinct from that other, included extreme. It is, then, sufficiently apparent that there is no kind of distinction which does not fall into one of the three classes mentioned above.

25. The only objection that could arise would be this: besides a distinction between thing and thing and between thing and mode, a distinction can be apprehended between mode and mode. Many think this is the case as regards subsistence and existence or, with greater reason, as regards subsistence and local presence. These modes cannot be mentally distinct, because they so exist in the real order as to have different principles and produce different modifications; also, they can be separated. These are signs of an actual distinction existing in nature, as we shall show presently. On the other hand they are not really distinct, for they are not distinct as thing from thing, seeing that they are not properly things. This is the argument we employed to prove that a mode is not really distinct from the thing it modifies. But neither can they be said to be only modally distinct, because one is not the mode of the

---

[31] Suarez here refers to "caput secundum" in "summa tertia" of the Junta edition, IV, text 52, fol. 15 vb 51-62, that is, *Physica*, I, 6, 189a 32-34.

other, and because they are often mutually separable from each other, which surely is a sign of a distinction greater than modal, as we shall explain directly.

26. *The distinction between two modes.* The reply to this objection is as follows. Since such modes do not possess being or entity except from the thing or in the thing to which they adhere, the manner in which they are distinct from other modes is to be judged in the light of this thing. But in any case the distinction between them will always pertain either to a real or to a modal distinction, supposing of course that they exist in a thing. I make this reservation because it is possible to conceive of modes that are only mentally distinct; in the same way that the mind can distinguish a single thing by means of inadequate concepts it can distinguish a single mode, as is the case very probably with action and passion, motion and time, existence and duration, and so on. But speaking of modes that are distinct in the thing itself, such as are local presence and the subsistence of human nature, I observe that these are compared with one another either as they exist in the same thing, or as modifying different things. If they are compared only according as they exist in the same thing, they are merely modally distinct, for the reason previously alleged: since they have no proper entity of themselves, they have of themselves nothing whereby they can be more than modally distinct. Nor do they possess a greater distinction in virtue of the thing they modify, since we are supposing that this is one and the same thing. Consequently they have no greater than a modal distinction.

By way of confirmation we may add that each of these modes has a certain identity with the thing it modifies, and hence in that thing and through that thing they have some sort of identity with each other; and so they retain only a modal distinction. Therefore it makes no difference that they can be mutually separated, that is, that one can persist without the other existing and vice versa, since it is necessary that at least the thing with which each mode is in some way identified continue to exist.

On the other hand, if modes which modify different things are compared, whether they are of the same order, such as two subsistences of two men, or of different orders, such as the sitting position of one man and the subsistence of the other, then the distinction between the modes is real, not of course by reason of the modes themselves, but by reason of the things in which they exist. For each of these modes has some sort of identity with the thing it modifies, and the things in question are really distinct from each other; consequently the modes also, and by reason of the things.

This conclusion is greatly strengthened by the consideration that these modes are mutually separable from each other, and that each is separable from the thing which the other modifies. This is a convincing sign of a

[36]

real distinction. And so all distinctions, even that between the modes themselves, are reducible to the above-mentioned three.

Objections Answered

27. The arguments advanced by the upholders of the first opinion,[32] so far as they can be urged against the modal distinction proposed by us, deserve a hearing.

First objection. With regard to the first objection,[33] the argument derived from real or mental being to infer a real or mental distinction can be understood in two senses. First, it can be understood as proceeding from the proper nature and cause of the distinction, so that a distinction would be held to be of the same kind as are the things on which the distinction hinges. Taken in this sense the argument is fallacious. For it has been shown that a mental distinction can intervene between real extremes, and conversely that at least a certain imitation of a real distinction can intervene between extremes in the mental order. Secondly, the argument can proceed from a consideration of proportion or parity: since in the realm of being there are no entities other than real or mental, so neither in the realm of distinctions can there be a middle ground between real and mental distinction.

If this proportion is rightly applied the argument can be granted; but it proves nothing conclusive against our doctrine. If real being is understood in its most 'comprehensive idea, as embracing everything that is not absolutely nothing and that can exist in reality otherwise than as a figment of the intellect, it is quite true that there is no medium between real and mental being; and in this same sense I admit that there is no medium between real and mental distinction. For every distinction based on the nature of the case can be termed real in this sense. Nearly all the ancient authors used the terms in this way.

But there is another sense in which real being can be understood, namely as that which of its own proper concept, or in virtue of what it formally is, can affect or constitute entity properly so called. In this sense it is false that there can be no medium between real and mental being. For there is a mode of being which is neither a mere entity of the mind, as is self-evident, nor a real being taken in the restricted and proper sense explained. Accordingly there is also a modal distinction which is intermediate between a mental distinction and a real distinction taken in this narrow sense.

28. *Second objection.* To the second objection[34] I reply that between "the same" and "other" understood univocally there is no medium, as

---

32 See no. 9 above.
33 See no. 10 above.
34 *Loc. cit.*

[37]

the argument rightly proves. However, understood according to various formalities, factors that are the same in one respect can be diverse in another respect, as St. Thomas says in the *Summa*, 1a, q. 1., a. 1, ad. 2. Thus being and mode can be said to be the same in reality, and nevertheless to involve a modal distinction in the concrete thing.

29. *Third objection.* Nor does the third objection[35] in any way militate against this. For we do not say that a thing and its mode are distinct according to their proper concepts, to the exclusion of any common predicate, as most of the examples there alleged suppose. In the same way that being and mode are objectively distinct, all superior predicates, even the transcendentals included in a mode, are distinct from whatever is included in the thing of which it is the mode. And so it must be conceded that, so far as a mode is an entity, the mode itself and the thing it modifies are two beings which are distinct in the real order or, loosely speaking, are really distinct.

However, we insist that a mode is not properly and strictly a being, and in this sense we deny that we have here two beings. Hence we flatly deny that being as properly understood is a predicate superior to a thing and its mode. Consequently there is no necessity, owing to the distinction between mode and thing, for multiplying beings understood in the proper and strict sense.

As regards the confirmatory reason advanced to support the third objection, the same is to be said of accident as was said of being: accident at times means a form having its own entity that of itself is really distinguishable and separable from every other entity; at times it means only the mode of another thing, whether this be an accident or a substance. If accident is understood in the first sense, the apprehension of several accidental natures in the same accident involves a contradiction, as the argument proves. But it is not contradictory for one accidental entity to have one or more modes only modally distinct from it.

But a substance simply as such does not signify a mode, but a thing properly so called and perfect in its own being; and the same is true of a body, and of any grade of substance classified under these headings. Therefore it is impossible to multiply such grades in the thing itself without multiplying things and substances. Nevertheless even in the realm of substance in general, or of substance analogously understood, there can be certain substantial modes; and within the same thing or substance strictly and simply as such it is possible for one or more substantial modes to be modally distinct from one another and from that substance; examples would be subsistence, union, and the like.

---

[35] See no. 11 above.

30. *Fourth objection.* After these remarks the solution to the fourth objection[36] is obvious; for what has been said of being is applicable to real essence. Essence can mean strictly a nature sufficient of itself to constitute an entity in the real order, or, more widely, any real principle that is constitutive of real being or mode. In this latter sense we concede that there are distinct essences in a thing and in a mode, and hence that objectively there is between them a distinction which in some sense is a real distinction. But as understood in the former sense there is a only one essence in any given entity; the modes which are objectively but modally distinct from the entity cannot be of its essence, but either are accidents or at most pertain in some way to its integrity or causality, as we shall explain later when discussing particular cases.[37]

From this it follows, as is to be carefully noted, that in any entity properly so called there is only one essential nature — and this at least is established by the proofs given at the start — which is, so to speak, fundamental and invariable in the entity, so that it is impossible for such an entity to be preserved in the real order without that essential nature, since this is what primarily constitutes it. Hence the entity must be specifically one, as the arguments prove. But modal factors, which can, as it were, adhere in or be affixed to such an entity, can be multiplied and diversified; for although they are in a thing they are outside its essence, as will appear more clearly in detail throughout the whole of our *Metaphysics.*

---

[36] See no. 12 above.
[37] E.g., Disp. XIII, sect. 9, no. 13; Disp. XVI, sect. 1, no. 13; Disp. XXXII, sect. 1, nos. 14-16; Disp. XXXIV, sect. 4, nos. 23-38; Disp. XXXVII, sect. 2, nos. 7-11

THE SIGNS OR NORMS FOR DISCERNING
VARIOUS GRADES OF DISTINCTION IN THINGS

1. *The Problem.* The whole difficulty consists in discriminating between a modal distinction and other distinctions. Real distinctions and mental distinctions are easily differentiated, since they are extreme opposites. But a modal distinction, being intermediate, is sometimes regarded as a real distinction, because of its similarity with the latter; at other times it is held to be nothing in reality, and is regarded as existing only in the mind, owing to the fact that it has certain points in common with mental distinctions. That we may have some general signs that can be applied to particular instances, I shall briefly propose a number of norms.

Throughout this discussion it is assumed that we discriminate between some objects with a distinction greater than that of the reasoning reason. Nothing further need be said of this distinction, as it is entirely a product of the mind. At the very least, or indeed first of all, the things to be distinguished must be capable of representation by distinct objective concepts, and they must exhibit formalities that are in some way distinct according to such concepts. Unless they are conceived at least in this way they will not be conceived as distinct, nor will there be any point to inquiring how great a distinction or what kind of distinction there may be between them. But once we suppose several objective concepts, we may with good reason inquire how we may know whether in actuality there is a distinction between them, and what kind it is.

The Sign of an Actual Distinction in the Real Order

2. First of all, I submit that whenever two objective concepts are capable of separation in nature and in the concrete individual, either in such a way that one can remain in the sphere of reality without the other, or in such a way that one is really disjoined from the other and that the real union between them is dissolved, we have a sign that the distinction between them is greater than a distinction of the reasoned reason. Consequently some sort of actual distinction is found in the thing itself, a distinction that is objective.

This is the common teaching of the doctors, and comes down from Aristotle, *Topics,* Bk. VII, chap. 1, locus 15,[38] where he says: "Moreover, if one thing can exist without the other, the former will not be the same as the latter." Alexander of Aphrodisias notes the same. It can also be derived from St. Augustine, *De Trinitate,* VI, 6,[39] where

---

[38] *Topica.* VII. 1, 152b 34-35. Junta, I, fol. 309 ra 14-16.
[39] *PL,* XLII, 928.

after stating, "In any given body magnitude, color, and figure are different things," he subjoins the proof: "The same color and the same figure can persist although the size is diminished, and with a change of color the same size and figure can persist. And although the figure does not remain the same, the body can remain as large as it was, and be colored in the same way, and other attributes simultaneously predicated of a body can individually and severally be changed without a change in the remaining attributes. Thus it is evident that the nature of a body is multiplex, and by no means simple." Farther on he proves that the human soul is not simple, since it has various acts and affections which he shows are distinct, "because some of these can be found without others, and some to a greater, others to a lesser extent."

The Scholastics, too, frequently apply this norm. Thus Peter Lombard, I *Sent.*, d. 8; Durandus, d. 30, q. 2; Scotus, *In II Sent.*, d. 1, q. 5 and *In III Sent.*, d. 8, q. 1; Ockham, *In I Sent.*, d. 1, q. 3, and Gabriel Biel, the same *Distinction*, q. 3, a. 3, dub. 1; Hervaeus, *Quodl. III*, q. 3. Among the commentators on Aristotle's *Metaphysics* this norm is used by John of Ghent, *Metaph.*, VI, q. 10; Anthony Trombeta, *Metaph.*, V, q. 3, a. 1; Fonseca, *Metaph.*, V, c. 6, q. 6, sect. 1. Similarly Ferrariensis, *Phys.*, I, q. 10; Paul of Venice, *Phys.*, text. 19; and Astudillo, as cited in the preceding section.[40] Many employ this rule to prove a distinction based on the nature of the case between subsistence and created nature; thus Giles of Rome, cited above,[41] and Medina, in his commentary on the *Summa*, IIIa, q. 4, a. 2. We will have occasion to mention others below. The same argument is often used to prove that the inherence of an accident is distinct from its existence, and that dependence or action is distinct from its term. But all this we shall see in the sequel.

3. This doctrine is demonstrated by a simple process of reasoning. If things conceived by us as having two objective concepts are joined together in reality and are subsequently separated, either each of them remains in existence after separation from the other, or one of them ceases to be, while the other remains.

In the former supposition these two are objectively, even really, distinct. The first reason for this is that it is impossible for the same thing to be altogether disjoined and separated from itself in the real order; an open contradiction is involved, since no greater union can be thought of than total identity in nature. This is not merely union, but unity. As it is impossible for the indivisible to be divided, so it is impossible for what is wholly the same to be separated from itself. Secondly, if these two remain in existence without being united to each other, one is not the mode of the other, and vice versa. For, as we have

---

40 No. 19.
41 *Loc. cit.*

[41]

seen, it is characteristic of a mode to be actually united or attached to the thing it modifies. Therefore whenever one thing can be separated from another and be preserved in its separated state, an evident sign is at hand that it is not the mode of that other. Accordingly it will either be a thing that of itself is really distinct from the other, or it will be a mode of another, really distinct thing. In consequence of this distinction the mode itself will be really distinct from the other thing.

But if two things are actually separated in such a way that one continues in existence but the other does not, they must be at least modally distinct. For, in the first place, the same thing cannot both be and not be. Hence if what previously existed no longer exists, whereas there is something that continues to exist, they cannot be altogether the same; otherwise the same thing would simultaneously exist and not exist. Secondly, when these two are separated, what is taken away and ceases to be is something positive (using the term "something" in the sense of whatever is opposed to nothingness, whether it be a thing or a real mode). Such, we are supposing, is each of the extremes that are separable in the aforesaid manner. Accordingly that positive something does not exist after separation; therefore when it was in existence it was in some way distinct from that which continues to exist. Finally, it is no less impossible for the same thing to be wholly separated from itself when one extreme is destroyed, than it was when both were preserved in existence; but it has been shown that the same thing cannot be separated from itself when the other extreme remains; therefore neither can it be separated from itself when the other extreme does not remain. Hence whenever such a separation can take place, a distinction in objective reality is supposed.

Greatly in error, therefore, are they who think that a relation is a real and positive something without which the foundation of the relation can remain in a thing, but is not actually and objectively distinct from the foundation. This involves an evident contradiction. For if a relation is in its essence something real, and at first exists in its foundation whereas later it does not, although the foundation remains unimpaired in its entity and essence, the relation, whatever it may be, must in some way be objectively distinct from the foundation. Otherwise what is wholly the same in reality would both cease to be and would remain.

4. *An objection answered.* You will object: animal is in fact conjoined to man, but as found in a horse or a lion is separable from man; nevertheless animal is not in objective reality distinct from man, as was shown above.[42] I reply that this is why, in proposing the norm, I insisted on the words: "what is capable of separation in nature and in the con-

---

[42] E.g., in Disp. VI, sect. 9, nos. 12, 17, 26. .

[42]

crete individual." Animal (and the same is true of all like predicates) is separable from man only according to the universal idea conceived in the mind, whereby it has unity in multiplicity not in objective reality, but only in the mind. But animal as joined to man in reality and in the individual is not separable from man; for this individual animal which in reality is this man cannot remain in the world of nature unless the man remains, just as, conversely, this man cannot continue in existence unless this animal also continues.

5. *Discussion of a theological instance. The divine relations in no way really distinct from the divine essence.* Perhaps you will insist: in God, at any rate, the divine essence, although numerically identical with the paternity, is separable from it inasmuch as the essence is united to the divine filiation; yet in objective reality they are not actually distinct. Because of this difficulty some theologians apparently admit an actual distinction, which in objective reality is at least modal, between a divine relation and the divine essence. This view is generally attributed to Scotus, but appears more clearly in Durandus; for Scotus speaks of his formal distinction in very obscure and general terms. This opinion, however, as presented above, is most erroneous, and is greatly opposed to the divine simplicity and perfection. We leave this controversy to theologians, and shall give but a brief reply.

First, I deny that the divine essence is separable from the paternity. It is one thing for the divine essence to be communicable to the [Son in] filiation or to the [Holy Spirit in] procession, but quite another for it to be separable from the paternity; rather, of its very nature the divine essence must be so communicated to the Son in filiation and to the Holy Spirit in procession that it is not separated from the Father in His paternity. Hence the norm of separation as proposed has no application here.

I reply, secondly, that to be thus communicable to several Persons really distinct from one another, without any other distinction from what is common to them than a mental or virtual distinction, is proper to a thing that is simply infinite. And so, using the term "separation" in the wide sense of conjunction with another thing that is really distinct, among creatures separation is an excellent argument to show that whatever is united with another really distinct thing is itself objectively distinct from the other extreme, since a finite thing, while it remains numerically the same, cannot be united by identity with things really distinct from it. But in an infinite thing this is no argument, because of its supreme simplicity and perfection. And this is the mystery of the Trinity, which we hold with unwavering certainty by faith alone.

6. I submit, secondly, that separation of one thing from another, if the separation is merely non-mutual (as it is commonly called), that is, a separation in which one extreme can remain without the other, but not conversely, is a convincing argument for a modal distinction, but not for a greater distinction, namely a real distinction in the technical sense. The first part of this proposition has been sufficiently established in the preceding assertion. The latter part is proved as follows.

A non-mutual separation rightly argues that the thing which can survive the destruction of the other extreme has of itself its own reality intrinsically and entitatively or essentially independent of the extreme which can be destroyed though the first thing remains. From this, however, we cannot conclude that the extreme which is capable of destruction has of itself its own proper entity, since, according to the supposition, that extreme is of such a nature that it cannot exist without the other. But to exist thus it suffices that it be the mode of the other. Indeed, as we have said, it is intrinsic to a modal entity that it cannot exist by itself or be actually separated from what it modifies. From such separation, therefore, a greater distinction than a modal distinction cannot be inferred. We may add as confirmation that local motion is in this way compared with a mobile object, and sitting with the sitter, and action with its terminus; but no one who regards the matter aright would require more than a modal distinction between such extremes.

7. *An important incidental question.* Admitting that this norm may be true negatively, that is, that a greater than modal distinction is not necessarily inferred from such separation, someone may ask whether the norm is also true positively, or in other words, whether extremes separable only in this way are invariably distinct with a mere modal distinction, so that a major or real distinction is excluded. Besides, such a rule is uncertain, and hence deceptive. For although this sign alone is not enough to prove a greater distinction, neither does it seem sufficient to warrant a denial of a greater distinction. It may be that the inseparability of the second extreme does not arise from any identity or minor distinction, but from some more intrinsic and separable mode of dependence. Thus, for example, a subject and its accident are so related that the subject can remain without the accident, but the accident cannot naturally remain without the subject, even though it is a thing distinct from the subject. And some authors are of the opinion that certain accidents, although they may be really distinct, cannot even supernaturally be conserved without their subject; such are vital acts, and perhaps there are other similar instances. Consequently the positive norm is either false or uncertain.

To this I answer that it is one thing to speak of natural inseparability, and another to speak of inseparability with reference to God's absolute power. From natural inseparability alone a convincing argument for a real indistinction in the strictest sense of the word cannot be derived, as the proposed objection shows, and also the example of subject and accident. And the same is true of matter and individual material forms. For matter can be separated from any particular form whatsoever, and can be conserved without the form; but no such form can be naturally separated from matter so as to endure without it.

8. *The objection met.* But if there is question of inseparability with reference to God's absolute power, a very probable argument can be constructed that extremes related in the manner described and incapable of existence in a state of mutual separation, are only modally distinct. The reason is that if one of these two extremes is of such a nature that it cannot be conserved without the other even by God's absolute power, this is a strong indication that it is essentially no more than some sort of mode rather than a true entity; if it were a true entity, it could not have so intrinsic a dependence on another entity that God could not supply for the dependence by His infinite power. This can be accounted for only by the fact that such an extreme is not an entity in its intrinsic essence, but is only a mode. The antecedent is evident, because God can supply for efficient causality as such, as is well known to all. Similarly, by maintaining an accident in being without its subject, He supplies for material causality (which is the only kind of causality that can come into question here), not with respect to the composite, but with respect to the other extreme. And in the same way, if the case should arise, He could supply for a corresponding formal causality, which is not of itself less intrinsic to a being than is material causality. Nor, to omit relation and its term, of which more presently, can any other kind of dependence between absolute things be imagined.

You will say: many think that matter cannot be conserved by God without form, even though form can be conserved without matter; but it does not follow that they are only modally distinct. I answer, let those who think thus reflect with what basis of probability they make such an assertion; this view could never meet with my approval, as I shall declare later when treating of causes.[43] Besides, the case is not similar as regards matter. For, even though we should grant for the sake of argument that matter cannot be preserved without some form, it certainly can be preserved naturally without this or that form or any particular form; and this is a sufficient proof that matter is not a mode of form, but is a distinct thing, as far as its own essence is concerned. For what is

---

[43] Disp. XV, sect. 9, nos. 3-10.

[45]

purely a mode not only cannot be separated from anything of which it is the mode, but this individual mode cannot be separated from this individual thing; for example, this position of sitting cannot be separated from this sitter. Therefore, since this numerically individual matter can be separated from this particular form and exist under some other form, we rightly conclude that it is not a mode of form. Again, from the fact that form is a separable thing and is able to endure without matter, at least by God's absolute power, we rightly conclude that it is not a mode of matter, but has its own entity in itself, an entity that is united to matter by a special union. Other arguments could be derived from the perfection of form over matter, from its activity, and other like considerations.

Accordingly the proposed norm, understood even in the positive sense, commends itself as highly probable, as far as our knowledge goes. I say, as far as our knowledge goes; because it might well be that some things distinct in themselves do not, to our knowledge, exhibit a sufficient sign of distinction. Since, then, we cannot pass judgment on things which are not perceived in themselves, except inasmuch as their effects or signs come to our attention, and since we have a general rule that distinctions are not to be multiplied without sufficient reason (seeing that a distinction does not occur in nature without a sufficient cause or without necessity), and lastly, since the inseparability in question seems directly to indicate some sort of identity, we conjecture with all probability that where a mutual separation is not possible, but only a non-mutual one, there is no distinction other than modal.

Signs of a Real Distinction

9. I state thirdly: although a number of signs are usually proposed to assist us in recognizing a real distinction, two of them, based on separation, seem the most important. One is based on separation alone, with reference to real union; that is, a distinction is real if both extremes can simultaneously and actually be preserved apart from a real union between them. The other is based on mutual separation with respect to existence; that is, a distinction is real if one extreme can be preserved immediately and by itself without the other, and vice versa, to the exclusion of any ordination to or necessary connection with a third thing. These two rules have been fairly well established by our explanation of the two preceding conclusions.

The first rule is evident, because the two things thus separated cannot be related in such a way that one is the mode of the other or vice versa; for the very essence of a mode demands that it cannot exist unless actually united to the thing it modifies, seeing that it is united by means of itself and not by some other mode of union, as has been amply

[46]

made clear. Consequently the two extremes will either be distinct things, as we are contending, or they will be modes of distinct things, or one will be a thing and the other the mode of another distinct thing. In all these cases they are really distinct, either by themselves or by reason of the distinct things, according to the doctrine of the preceding section.[44]

The second rule is established as follows. When two extremes are so related that they can be mutually separated, and that one of them can be preserved without the other, neither can be the mode of the other, since in virtue of its very nature a mode cannot exist apart from the thing it modifies; hence each of them is a genuine thing with a true entity that can be preserved without the other. Therefore extremes of this sort are of necessity really distinct; for they are distinct in objective reality, since they can be separated; they are distinct not merely as thing and mode of thing, but as thing and thing. Therefore they are really distinct. But, as I noted above, each must be capable of existing without the other by itself and immediately. For it is possible for two modes of the same thing to be capable of existing one without the other, and contrariwise. In this case a real distinction between the modes cannot be deduced, because there is a certain real identity between, not, formally speaking, by reason of what they are in themselves, but by reason of the thing they modify; besides, neither of them is separable in such a way as to be able to exist without the thing it modifies.

10. It is evident from all this that there is no point to inquiring whether such separation can take place naturally or only through God's absolute power. For to be actually affixed and to modify the thing of which it is the mode is so essential to what we call a pure mode, that not even by God's absolute can it be conserved without that thing or without actually modifying it. Thus figure cannot be even mentally conceived as separated from all quantity and from the thing of which it is the figure; or a relation from its foundation, if it is the mode of the foundation; or motion from the mobile object; and so of similar instances.

The reason for this was touched on above. Such modes of their very concept lack sufficient entity to sustain them; they have entity only by reason of a certain identity with the things in which they exist. Hence whatever is separable in the manner described, even though the absolute power of God were to intervene, is not a mode but a distinct thing. With regard, then, to inferring a distinction in the thing itself, it makes no difference whether the separation take place naturally or supernaturally. As far as our own perception is concerned, a distinction will be more easily recognized if the separation occurs naturally. Now and then, to be

---
[44] No. 26.

[47]

sure, separation is brought to our notice by supernatural mysteries, the knowledge of which is a great aid to an understanding of natural things. Thus through the mystery of the Eucharist we are made more certain that quantity is a thing distinct from substance than would be possible through purely natural contemplation.

11. *A point worthy of attention.* In this connection we may observe in passing that even though a mutual separation and conservation of two things is not effected, but only a separation of one from the other, this enables us to infer a real distinction. Thus in the example just given, God has not, so far at least, caused a material substance to remain in being without quantity, but has only caused quantity to endure without a material substance; yet this is a sufficient argument enabling us to conclude that quantity and substance are not only modally, but really distinct. This is so not because of the form (if I may speak thus), but because of the matter. For in the case of human nature and subsistence it has been brought about that human nature is conserved without created subsistence; but it has not been brought about, nor do we believe it can be, that created subsistence should exist without its own substantial nature of which it is the term. Hence in this case we do not infer a real distinction from the separation, but only a modal distinction.

Accordingly in such instances, besides separation we must consider the nature of that which is maintained in being without the other extreme. It may seem to be joined to this other extreme by its very nature, and to be less perfect than the latter, and also to be quite capable of verifying the notion of a mode; but if, in spite of all this, it is conserved without the other extreme, we have a sign of a real distinction. The case is different when that which remains in being is the more perfect, and has the principal entity of the thing.

Thus in the examples given, comparison of substance with quantity makes it clear that substance is the more perfect, so that if one had to be the mode of the other, substance would not be the mode of quantity, but rather quantity would have to be the mode of substance. But since separation of quantity from substance clearly reveals that quantity is not a mode but a true thing, the consequence quite logically follows that substance and quantity are not distinguished as thing and mode, but as two things. In the case of nature and subsistence, on the contrary, it appears that substantial nature is the principal entity of the thing, and that if either of them is the mode of the other, subsistence is the mode of the nature, and not the other way around. Here the separation effected does not show that subsistence is more than a mode, since it is not conserved without the nature. Therefore we are not justified in concluding from such separation that there is a real distinction, but only that there is a modal distinction.

12. *The ascertainment of a distinction between extremes which no power has yet caused to exist in a separated state.* A difficulty remains: when no separation has been effected either naturally or supernaturally, how can a real distinction be recognized? The rules established above can be of no service. Yet many things that have not thus far been separated in any of the ways mentioned may well be really distinct, such as the matter and form of celestial bodies. If you contend that even if they have not been separated, they can still be recognized as separable, this is the same as saying that they are perceived to be distinct; at any rate the difficulty remains the same. For this precisely is the object of our inquiry — *how* we can know that they are separable, if they are not separated by natural means, and have not thus far been separated by God in any of the ways indicated.

The difficulty grows when we reflect that some things are inseparable even by God's absolute power, and yet are held to be really distinct. Many maintain that this is the case with the intellect and the will, as regards their distinction from each other and also from the soul. In view of the prior difficulty, then, we may say that the proposed sign based on separation is neither adequate, nor is it the only norm, nor is it always primary and necessary, but is assigned as more certain and recognizable only when it can be applied. Accordingly several other signs are proposed, and so we must briefly consider them.

A Sign of Real Distinction Rejected as Useless

13. The first of these complementary signs is the distinction of existences: things that are really distinct have distinct existences: but things that are only modally distinct have only one existence. For a mode is a mode precisely because it has no other existence than the existence of the thing it modifies.

14. But this sign is worthless. Either it is more obscure than the object of our investigation, or it begs the question, or it involves some error. First of all, if it is true that existence is the actual entity of a thing, to say that those things are really distinct which have distinct existences, is the same as saying that those things are really distinct which have distinct entities. But if existence is imagined to be a thing distinct from actual essence, then either the supposition is that things having distinct existences also have distinct essences — and this is indeed true, but it is no less difficult to know distinct existences than to know distinct essences, unless perhaps through separation; or else it is asserted that two essences can have a single existence, and so are only modally distinct, whereas a real distinction occurs when a distinction of existences is joined to a distinction of essences — and this I judge not only to be so obscure that it cannot be naturally ascertained of any ob-

jects whatsoever, but further to be false, because there is no greater reason for distinguishing essences than existences in extremes that are modally distinct. For the same kind of distinction which occurs between essences can occur between existences. Accordingly, supposing for the present what we shall demonstrate later,[45] that existence is nothing else than the very entity of actual essence, then just as distinct existences are apprehended in a thing and in a mode, since the mode as condistinct from the thing it modifies has its own actuality, so the nature and kind of distinction between these two extremes will be the same whether they are considered in potency or in act, whether they are considered from the standpoint of essence or from the standpoint of existence.

Moreover, in the view that existence is a thing distinct from essence,[46] things that are really distinct can exist with one and the same indivisible existence; thus matter and form, and all the parts of the same composite. Hence according to this opinion a distinction between things is not sufficiently nor truly manifested by a distinction of existences, at least in those things which are distinct but united to one another. But it is with these that the present difficulty is chiefly concerned, in the theory that distinct things can have the same existence. If anyone will refuse to admit this conclusion, he can have no reason for logically admitting that a thing and a mode have absolutely the same existence, but one which is at the same time modally distinct, so that each extreme may have an existence suited to it. In a word, the question of the distinction between things or modes will be the same as the question of the distinction between existences.

Discussion of Another Sign of Real Distinction, taken from Aristotle

15. A second sign can be deduced from diverse production or corruption: that is, those things are said to be really distinct which are generated or corrupted by a different process of generation and corruption. On the other hand, those things are really the same which are generated by the same generation. This is the sign used by Aristotle, *Metaphysics*, Bk. IV, text. 3,[47] to prove that being and one are the same. This doctrine is referred to by Fonseca, following Anthony Trombeta, *De formalitatibus*, chap. 2. Fonseca attacks it, on the ground that the properties of the soul are produced along with the soul itself by [one and] the same action, but nevertheless are distinct things. Conversely, he points out, a relation is not really distinct from its foundation, nor figure from quantity, yet these are produced by different actions. However I do not think that this sign is false if it is understood rightly; but I do

---

[45] Cf. Disp. XXXI, sect. 4-7.
[46] Suarez seems never to have rightly grasped the Thomistic teaching on essence and existence.
[47] *Metaphysica*, IV, 2, 1003b, 22-23 Junta VIII, fol. 31 vb 32-33.

think it is practically useless for discerning a distinction, except inasmuch as in some way it includes the sign of separation.

Let me explain in detail. I take for granted that there is question only of a natural action or production of things, so that matters are not complicated by the introduction of miracles. Further, I assume that there is question of things which by their very nature require distinct actions for their production, even if they are produced simultaneously. The reason for these assumptions will be explained below.[48] Moreover, I observe, the statement that some things are produced by distinct actions can be understood in two senses: first, things can be produced in such a way that each is produced by an action primarily directed to it, *without* any natural connection or orderly succession between such actions; secondly *with* an interconnection between the actions, so that one results from the other with natural necessity. Likewise, there are two ways of understanding the assertion that some things are produced by one and the same action: that is, things are either produced with equal primacy and without the derivation of one from another, or one is produced primarily and another secondarily, in the sense that the latter product results necessarily from the former.

16. Accordingly, things produced in the first way, that is, primarily for their own sakes, by actions that are really distinct, must themselves be really distinct. Understood in this sense, the proposed norm is quite trustworthy. For the nature and distinction of actions are judged from their terms; hence if the terms are such as to require distinct actions for their production, they themselves will be distinct. However, we cannot absolutely infer a real distinction between the terms from this fact, indeed we cannot infer any distinction greater than that obtaining between the actions themselves. These can at times be really distinct, as for example the production of wood and the heating of it. But at times they are only modally distinct, as in the case of the production of wood and its local motion; these actions are distinct solely as two modes of the same wood. Things produced by such actions are distinct in the same way; for the former actions produce substance and heat, which are really distinct; but the latter produce substance and *Ubi* or local presence, which are only modally distinct. Hence things produced preserve a distinction conformable to the actions which produce them.

This is true not only when such actions take place separately and without any natural connection, as is the case with the production and the heating action of fire, but also when these actions are naturally joined and when one results from the other. This would happen, for instance, in the production of some heavy object in the atmospheric

---

[48] In no. 18 of this section.

regions, and the same object's downward motion which would naturally follow upon such generation. Here evidently, and almost with sense perception, there is a distinction between the actions, since one takes place intrinsically in a single instant, whereas the other begins only extrinsically in the same instant.

However the same distinction and logical succession are possible with instantaneous actions, for example, the production of fire and the succeeding heat. This is true likewise of the production of the soul and the emanations of its potencies therefrom; for if these potencies are distinct things, the derivation, too, is an action physically distinct, although it results from the other action, the production, and hence cannot be said to take place primarily for itself. Similar examples can be adduced in the case of actions that are only modally distinct, such as the creation of an angel and the production of some *Ubi* or local presence, which naturally follows upon creation; or the production of some quantity and its subsequent figuration; likewise the production of a foundation for a relation and the resulting relation, supposing that the relation is a distinct mode. Thus it is clear that the instances or examples urged against this doctrine possess no force; for in all these cases the distinction between the actions corresponds to the distinction between the terms, and conversely.

17. As to Aristotle's principle in the passage cited, namely that products generated by one and the same production are the same, the sense in which it is true stands forth clearly. It is true of things produced per se and immediately, by a single real action. But products that are only said to be produced, or rather are co-produced by one action, inasmuch as one results from another. need not be really the same; it suffices that they be the same in their subject, or in some bond of union, since in reality they are not produced immediately and proximately by one real action. as has been shown in the case of substance and its really distinct passions. Indeed, this one action must be understood as indivisible; for if it is in any way composite, some distinction will be perceivable in its adequate term. For example, by the single action of heating, or by the eduction of a form from the potency of matter, heat or a form is produced and is united to the subject or to matter. Thus in the term are produced two effects which are distinct by the nature of the case, or modally, namely the entity and the union of the form or of heat. Yet the action is one, although it is in some fashion composed of the quasi-partial modes which can be discerned in it.

18. It is also manifest from what has been said why I stated that this sign is practically useless for recognizing distinctions in things. For the same kinds of distinctions can be found between actions as between

their terms, namely real, modal, and occasionally mental, such as the distinction between the generation of a man and an animal (in the same human being.) But these kinds of distinction are not more clearly perceived by us in actions than in the terms of actions. Indeed, more often and by natural impulse we begin our search for a distinction in actions by inspecting their terms. Thus we judge that heating is an action really distinct from wood, but that its collocation in such and such an *Ubi* is only modally distinct, for no other reason than the fact that heat is a distinct thing, whereas local presence is only a distinct mode.

Moreover, I added, all this is to be understood of a distinction in actions which the terms of their very nature require; for if the actions are distinct merely by temporal succession or by the various ways in which they take place, it does not necessarily follow that any distinction in the term is inferred from the distinction between the actions. Just as distinct modes can exist in the same thing, especially if they are successive, so distinct actions can tend to the same term, although they proceed from distinct agents, or occur at different times. Thus the illumination now produced by one action of one lamp can subsequently be sustained by another lamp through a distinct action; and the same man who is produced by generation is reproduced by resurrection.

Lastly, I insisted that miracles must not be brought in to complicate matters, because the divine power can produce or conserve the same object by several actions, not only successively but simultaneously, as I showed at greater length in the third volume of my commentary on the Third Part of the *Summa*.[49] On the other hand, I do not think it possible for things wholly distinct to be produced by one and the same action. The reason for this difference is not hard to perceive in view of what has been established. For an action is a certain mode of the thing that is produced; but one and the same indivisible mode cannot exist in distinct things, as has been demonstrated above.[50] But the existence of several modes in the same thing involves no contradiction, as long as the modes themselves are not mutually exclusive. Of course this might seem superfluous when the modes are of the same nature, or have the same function; still, with respect to the divine wisdom it is possible that they would not be superfluous. At any rate there is apparent no repugnance that would make this impossible.

Examination of Another Sign of Real Distinction

19. A third sign is in common use; that is, when we have one thing producing and another thing produced, we have a sufficient sign of a real distinction. Thus Fonseca, *Metaph.*, chap. 6, q. 6, sect. 1, with

49 Vol. XIX of the Vivès edition. Disp. XLIV, sect. 5; sect. 6, no. 9 f.; cf. Vol. XXI, Disp. XLIX, sect. 1, nos. 6-8.
50 See sect. 1, nos. 20, 26; sect. 2, no. 6.

a reference to St. Thomas, *Summa,* Ia, q. 41, a. 4. But in the first place this is not a universal sign, as is self-evident. Secondly, if it is brought forward merely for inferring a distinction from the nature of the case, prescinding from the question whether it is modal or properly real, it is in general true. But if it is understood of a real distinction in the technical meaning, then, to be trustworthy, it must be restricted either to a production that is substantial in the proper, perfect, and primary sense, or to a production that is accidental but that terminates in something which is not united to the producing cause. In these two cases a real distinction is always required; in others, not always.

That a real distinction is always required in a substantial production is evident; one and the same substantial suppositum cannot properly and primarily produce itself, since it must be assumed to exist before it can produce. Hence if it produces a suppositum, it produces one distinct from itself. Even the divine Persons, although they have unity in their essence, are really distinct on account of the real production of one from another. Note that I said, "properly and primarily"; for perhaps it is possible for a thing to reproduce itself by a miracle. Yet in such a contingency the thing in question must be supposed to have first been produced by a different action, and hence the second action is not a primary production, nor is it a production properly so called, but a production only by way of conservation; but of this we shall speak at greater length in the treatise on the Eucharist.[51]

The case of accidental production may be explained as follows. Whatever is produced by another, must be actually distinct from that other in objective reality, since even the production itself must in some sense be distinct from the producer, especially when it is an accidental production. Hence also its term must be objectively distinct from the producing thing. Accordingly, in the supposition that such a term is not produced in union and conjunction with the producing cause, it cannot be a mode of the latter, but must be a thing distinct from it, or a mode of a thing distinct from it. Therefore the thing produced must be not only modally but really distinct from the producing thing, either immediately by itself, or by reason of the thing in which it exists. But if the production is accidental, and terminates in something that is united and joined to the producing cause, we lack a sufficient sign of a real distinction. Sometimes, indeed, such a distinction can intervene, as when the sense of sight produces vision, and so of the intellect, the will, and similar faculties, which produce qualities really distinct from themselves, whereby the faculties themselves are informed. But this is not absolutely necessary, as is evident whenever what is produced is only a mode of

---

[51] Vol. XXI of the Vivès edition, Disp. L, sect. 4, nos. 10-16.

the producing thing, whether it is produced per se and by a proper action, as in local presence which he who moves effects in himself, or whether it is produced only by a resulting action, as in the emanation of subsistence from nature, and in like cases. If it should be asserted that a real distinction between producer and product is inferred not from any kind of production whatsoever, but only from a production that is a thing distinct from the producing cause, the argument will ramble uselessly in a vicious circle. We cannot conclude that such an action is a thing distinct from the producing cause otherwise than from the fact that the action produces not some mode of the producing thing, but a true quality or a form affecting it; but this precisely was the object of the inquiry.

20. The same judgment is to be passed on another sign which the same author proposes in the context cited, on the relation between cause and effect. There is place for this sign mainly in efficient causality, of which there is question throughout this discussion; but with due modification all the arguments advanced can be applied to formal or material causes. Although most properly the doctrine is not verified except with regard to act and potency which are really distinct, it admits of some application in the case of a modifying mode and the thing modified. There is no place, however, for the sign in final causality, since end and effect can coincide in the same thing; so also can end and agent, or end and form.

21. *Conclusion from this discussion.* Therefore a sure sign of a real distinction is hardly forthcoming when things are such that naturally they are always and necessarily found to be really united to one another, and have not thus far been separated by divine intervention. I do not deny that many things of this kind may be found to be really distinct, as is clear from the examples mentioned above.[52] I am merely pointing out that we lack a universal sign for discerning such a distinction. We must examine each instance in the light of the essential nature proper to it, its degree of perfection, and the function to which it is ordained, so that from all these together we may form a judgment on the distinction.

Thus we readily admit a real distinction between the matter and form of celestial bodies, because we know from our general understanding of the nature of matter and form that neither is a mode, but a true entity. Moreover, from the various properties exhibited by a celestial body we apprehend that matter and form are found therein according to their proper concepts. Lastly, from their limited perfection we conclude that they are distinct by the nature of the case, and hence are really distinct.

---

[52] Cf., e.g., sect. 2, no. 12.

Similarly a real distinction is believed to exist between a substantial form and a potency that of itself is primarily ordained to the production of an accidental act, because the nature of an operative faculty is very perfect in its own kind. Hence such a potency does not seem to be some accidental mode, which ordinarily is most imperfect, but a true entity and a form ordained of itself to the production of such an act. On the other hand, considering the limitations of a finite substance, its essential nature, as it exists in reality, does not seem to comprehend such diverse notions or aptitudes for acts so diverse as are the acts of being and operating. Hence we conclude that between substantial form and active potency there is a real distinction, since it is a distinction not between a thing and a mode, but between essences that constitute proper entities.

And this is the way we must reason in all other cases, examining, first, whether those natures between which a distinction is sought exceed the notion of a mode, and whether each is of itself sufficient to constitute an entity; and then, whether the diversity between them appears so great as to require in the finite thing itself some objective and actual distinction. Thus a probable conjecture as to the quality of the distinction becomes possible.

A Doubt Concerning the Separability of Distinct Things

22. *Things really distinct are capable of mutual separation if they can continue in existence.* There remains a doubt, which was touched on in the second part of the proposed difficulty:[53] whether all things that are really distinct in objective nature can be separated by divine power. This question can be posed regarding the two kinds of separation briefly described above.[54] The first has to do only with the separation of things that had been really united, both extremes being capable of continued existence subsequent to separation. The second concerns separation with regard to existence, that is, a separation in which one of the extremes is destroyed, while the other remains in existence. I assume, of course, that the question turns upon things that are altogether distinct from each other, so that they are not related as whole and part, or container and contained; for of such things it is evident that what includes another cannot be preserved without that other, since it is intrinsically made up of lesser elements. With regard to things that are altogether distinct, various opinions could be reviewed, but I omit them, as they pertain to specialized questions.

Beginning, then, with the first kind of separation mentioned above, I contend that such things can always be thus separated by God's absolute power (which we are including in this discussion); nor is any ex-

---

[53] Sect. 2, no. 7 f.
[54] *Ibid.*, no. 9.

ception to be made in this matter. The reason is that in these things the mutual separation of one from the other cannot involve a contradiction arising from the defect of sufficient entity (as is the case with modes), since, in our supposition, each of them possesses true entity distinct from the other. Hence, if there were any contradiction, it could arise only from the dependence of one on the other, or from their natural connection or the derivation of one from the other. No other alternative can be thought of.

It is true that a natural inseparability can rightly be inferred from, such dependence or connection; but the same is not true with reference to God's absolute power. For, as was indicated above,[55] God can supply for all such dependence in the order of efficient causality. If the dependence is in the order of formal or material cause, we are restricting the question to such formal or material causality as does not intrinsically constitute being, but sustains or actuates a thing distinct from the cause, that is, a causality which is known as extrinsic in some way. But God can supply for all this. More easily still God can prevent all natural derivation, both because such derivation is impossible without God's concurrence, which He can refuse to give, and because He can destroy any union between the two things in question, and effect or preserve each of them by His sole power.

And so in this matter I find neither a general contradiction nor any reasonable exception. Some authors introduce an exception in the case of passions and essence. But their view either lacks all justification, or, if supported by some specious reasoning, this proves rather that the things are not really distinct, and not that, supposing a distinction, they are incapable of separation.

23. *Reply to an objection.* A difficulty can be urged only with regard to relations of union, such as the relations of matter and form. These relations are really distinct, as are matter and form themselves, in which they exist adequately. Nevertheless the relations cannot be preserved when separated, but only when united.

The answer to this is, first, that if there is question of predicamental relations, perhaps they are not something in nature really distinct from such a union, but are only a mutual denomination of things united to each other. Or, if we admit that these relations are positive real modes of united parts, the answer is that they are not united to each other, formally speaking, but are relations between united parts; the reason they cannot be preserved without the union between the parts is that they are based on that union. This is not against the doctrine we are defending.

---

[55] *Ibid.*, no. 8.

But if there is question of the formal union itself, which is relative by denomination or transcendentally, that union is not a thing distinct from the united parts, but is a mode of them. Hence it is not surprising that such a mode cannot survive the dissolution of the union itself, since the mode and the union are identical.

24. *One of two distinct things can be destroyed, while the other endures.* With regard to the second kind of separation, I maintain that in this case also distinct things can be separated by divine power, provided we make a threefold exception, which can be comprised under the single designation of essential ordination or dependence. The general reason for this norm has already been intimated. That is, if things are really distinct, they can also be really disjoined; and if they are really disjoined, no repugnance or contradiction is involved in the notion of one of them being preserved by God without the other. For invariably there can be between them only an effective dependence, not an essential dependence; and God can supply for this.

25. *First exception: God and creatures.* The first exception is that of creatures with respect to God. Creatures are things distinct from God, and God can exist without them, but they cannot exist without God; not only because God is necessary per se Being, but on account of the essential dependence of creatures on God. Hence even in the impossible supposition that there is no God, creatures could not exist without Him. But no creature has so essential an effective dependence on another creature, especially if it has the true entity and reality of which we are now speaking. I make this remark because what is intrinsically no more than a mode can, perhaps, essentially depend on the subject it modifies. But there is no need to discuss this here, since it is not pertinent to the present question.

26. *Second exception: relation and its term.* The second exception is that of relation and a really distinct term. Neither one can be sustained in the real order without the other, even though there is not properly a real union between them, but only an ordination. The reason is that a relation as such essentially and, as it were, formally depends on its term; hence it can neither arise nor be preserved without the term. The only argument for proving this is that such is the nature of a relation, as is now assumed in accordance with the doctrine commonly accepted; for we are speaking of a real relation that is purely predicamental.

27. *Third exception: the divine Persons.* The third example is that of the divine Persons who, though really distinct, cannot be separated from one another in being, because of the intrinsic and necessary con-

[58]

nection among them. To be convinced of this we have but to refer to the preceding number; they are relative Persons, and so one cannot be without another. This conclusion is likewise deduced from their union in essence by true and perfect identity with it, on account of which each of the Persons is simply necessary Being, so much so that it is absolutely and simply impossible for Him not to be. Consequently none of them can be without the others; for if it is impossible for any of the Persons to be without eternal existence, the conclusion follows that not a single one of them could be while another does not exist. For this reason too, creatures, although they do not per se depend on the divine relations as such, cannot be isolated in their being from these same relations. For creatures cannot exist except on the supposition that the divine relations exist, since these relations are simply necessary Being. And although from the creature's standpoint the divine relations are not per se necessary for its creation, they are necessary from God's standpoint, because they are per se in God, and essentially are God. Lastly, this truth is inferred formally and convincingly from the union of the relations with the divine essence by identity. For, since each of the divine relations and the essence are in reality altogether identical, the essence cannot exist in reality without each of the relations, nor can any of the relations exist without the essence. Hence not even one of the relations can exist without the others.

The objection might be made that this argument is based on the principle gathered from Aristotle, *Metaphysics*, Bk. IV, text. 3,[56] that things which are the same as a third thing are the same as each other — a principle which has no place in the Trinity; otherwise we should infer not only that one relation cannot exist without another, but that it is this other. In answer let me point out that the argument is not based formally on that principle, but either on the principle that things which are entirely the same in reality cannot be separated in such a way that one exists without the other; or certainly on the principle that the divine essence and relation are identical not in some indeterminate manner, but in such fashion that the divine essence is of the very essence of the relation, and the relation is the intrinsic terminus of the essence. Accordingly the relation cannot exist without the essence that is essential to it, nor can the essence exist without its intrinsic and absolutely necessary terminus. But enough of this for the present occasion.

---

[56] The axiom is nowhere explicitly formulated in *Metaphysica*, IV, text 3. Junta VII fol. 31 vb. 32-58. Cf. *Metaphysica*, IV, 2, 1003b 22-34. But it is an obvious application of the principle of contradiction, which Aristotle discusses throughout this book.

28. The way in which a mental distinction may be recognized and marked off from other kinds of distinction can readily be understood in the light of the foregoing doctrine. There is no difficulty about the distinction of the reasoning reason. Since this distinction not only does not exist in the object, but lacks even a foundation therein, it is very easily recognized. This is so especially as it does not imply a formal diversity in the objective concepts themselves, but only a quasi-material diversity by the repetition or comparison of the same concept which, though it is one, we employ as if it were many, as Aristotle indicates in *Metaphysics*, Bk. V, chap. 9, text. 16.[57] But the distinction of the reasoned reason requires some formal diversity in the objective concepts, and herein it differs from the distinction of the reasoning reason; and so it has this much in common with distinctions found in the real order. To decide that this is a mental distinction and not a real distinction, it is sufficient that, in addition to the distincton in concepts, none of the signs from among all those listed for the discernment of a modal or a real distinction be discovered. For, since distinctions are not to be multiplied without reason, and the sole distinction between concepts does not suffice for inferring a distinction in the thing, a distinction is always to be regarded as a mental distinction, and not a real distinction, whenever none of the signs of a greater distinction is joined to the mere distinction in the concepts.

Hence, I conclude, whenever it is quite clear that any two extremes, which are united and conjoined in a thing, are distinct in their objective concepts in such a way that in the concrete individual they are absolutely inseparable, both mutually and non-mutually, both by God's absolute power and by natural force, both as regards existence and as regards the real union between them, we have a sound and practically certain argument that they are not actually distinct in the object, but are distinct with a distinction of the reasoned reason. This is established by the foregoing doctrine, and in the first instance by induction. Thus Peter, man, animal, and other like predicates, as they really are in Peter, are not distinct in objective fact. In the intellect, similarly, the superior and the inferior reason, synderesis, memory, and like attributes, do not signify things distinct in reality, but only by the reasoned reason. For the faculty of intellect is such that, adequately considered, it comprehends all these, and they are not separable in any manner, even by God's absolute power, as far as regards the faculty itself, although they may be separated for convenient usage in speaking about them.

[57] *Metaphysica*, V, 9, 1018a 7-9. Junta VIII, fol. 56 rb 14-16.

The same doctrine is established, secondly, by the argument already suggested, namely that things which are of this nature do not seem to be inseparable for any other reason than that they have one indivisible essence and entity in the object; otherwise why could they not be separated at least by divine power, especially in creatures? The final reason is that here a sufficient sign of a greater distinction is lacking. Hence the distinction ought to be considered only mental, as long as a greater distinction is not evidently required.

COMPARISON OF "THE SAME" AND "OTHER"
BOTH WITH EACH OTHER AND WITH BEING

1. Aristotle treats of "the same" and "other" in his *Metaphysics*, Bk. V, chap. 9. Many place this attribute, which we said above is comprised under unity,[58] among the various passions of being. The doctrine is also based on Aristotle, *Metaphysics*, Bk. X, text. 9, and chap. 5 and 6.[59] And so, as we come to the end of these discussions on unity and multitude, we must treat briefly of "the same" and "other". Our purpose is to explain the usage of a number of terms in this science, rather than to contribute anything new. Whatever is pertinent to the doctrine has been dealt with in our treatises on the kinds of unity and distinctions.[60]

2. We must observe at the outset that "the same" can be spoken of in two senses, namely relatively and negatively; or (in the terminology of others) formally and fundamentally. And it is true that "the same", formally understood, seems to involve a relation, and in this chiefly it is distinguished from unity. But when we speak of "the same" negatively, we mean what is not diverse or distinct from another, almost in the sense in which "nothing" differs from "one", except that "one" implies a negation of division *in* itself, whereas "the same" implies a negation of division *from* itself, or from that object with which a being is said to be identical. For this reason Aristotle says, *Metaphysics*, Bk. V, chap. 9, text. 16,[61] that sameness is a kind of unity in being.

This is clear in that sameness whereby a person is said to be the same as himself. If this statement is taken relatively and formally, as it is understood in Aristotle, and as it ought to be understood in accord with common doctrine, it implies only a mental relation. For there can be no real relation of "the same" to itself, since there must be a true opposition between a relation and its term; but there can be no opposition between "the same" and itself. Nevertheless in this formal sense no one will be said to be the same as himself, that is, to be referred to himself with such a relation, except when he is thus conceived or compared in the mind. But without any comparison or intellectual fiction a person is said to be the same as himself fundamentally or negatively, since he is not diverse or divided from himself. In this latter sense same-

---

[58] Disp. III, sect. 2, no. 12.
[59] *Metaphysica* X, 3, 1054a 20-29. Junta, VIII, fol. 121 ra 59 to rb 8. Suarez's reference to chapters 5 and 6 is in Junta VIII, fol. 125 rb 18-127 va 69, that is *Metaphysica*, X, 6-7, 1056b 3-1057b 34.
[60] In Disputations IV-VII.
[61] *Metaphysica*, V, 9, 1018a 7. Junta VIII, fol. 56 rb 14-15: "idenitas unitas quaedam essentiae est."

ness can be numbered among the passions of being, although the negation in question can be attributed not only to a true being, but also to a fictitious being, not only to a being that is a unit in itself, but also to an aggregate, or multitude and number of beings. For any number is the same as itself, just as one or unity is.

In yet another sense Scotus distinguishes sameness into absolute and relative, as is reported by Hervaeus, *Quodl.* IV, q. 2; Soncinas, *Metaph.*, Bk. X, q. 3; and Javelli, in q. 7 of his commentary. Absolute sameness he calls that whereby a thing is said to be the same as itself, because in this case no reference to another thing is implied; and relative sameness he calls that whereby one thing is said to be the same as another. And, as the authors mentioned point out, Scotus contends that these two samenesses are really distinct, and in this they attack him. And truly, if we consider relative sameness between things that are distinct only by the reasoned reason, as are man and Peter, this opinion is deservedly assailed, because the identity of Peter with himself, or with man, or with animal does not differ in reality, but only as greater and less, according to our notions. Otherwise the extremes themselves would have to be distinct in reality. But if we consider relative sameness between things that are really distinct, and then compare the identity whereby Peter is the same as himself with the identity whereby he is the same as Paul, we can say that the identities are really diverse, since one is a sameness of thing, the other a sameness of reason. But as the doctrine itself is clear, there is no cause to quarrel about terminology.

3. We must observe, secondly, along with Aristotle in the passages cited above, that sameness is sometimes regarded in some one thing in itself or with respect to itself, sometimes in many things that are compared with one another, or in one thing as compared with another. In the first case Peter is said to be numerically the same as himself. In the second case he is specifically the same as Paul, or generically the same as a lion. In this sense Aristotle says, *Metaphysics*, Bk. V, chap. 9,[62] that those things are the same which are in some respect one, either in genus or in species or by some analogy. The first kind of sameness, if it is regarded from the standpoint of negation or its foundation, is sameness simply as such, just as is unity, because it is real sameness; regarded relatively, however, it is sameness only in a qualified sense, because the relation of sameness to itself is not real, but only mental. On the contrary, the sameness of several distinct things in a common notion (we are speaking of creatures, and are not touching on the identity of the three divine Persons in one numerical essence), if regarded from the standpoint of its foundation and the negation of division, is only

---

[62] *Metaphysica,* V, 9, 1018a 12-17. Junta VIII, text 16, fol. 56 rb. 21-29.

a sameness in a qualified sense, or rather it is a certain likeness, because it is only a unity in concept, as was shown above.[63] But with respect to relationship of identity, this sameness is held to be sameness simply as such, because the relation between distinct things is a real relation, according to the common teaching on relations, as we shall see later.[64]

All this is quite generally admitted, as far as doctrine goes. As concerns the usage of the terms involved, we should note that the conformity of several things in a common notion retains, in the case of substances, the simple name of sameness, by a consent of usage; in the case of qualities it is called likeness, in the case of quantity it is called equality, although this term signifies not only conformity in an essential notion, but also in size. In all these instances, however, there is the same formal concept of sameness, just as there is the same kind of unity; and so they are all included under "the same" and "other", as these are understood transcendentally and are attributed to being.

4. *The various kinds of sameness correspond in number to the kinds of distinction.* We must observe, thirdly, that when we speak of "the same" in the sense of a denial of division either from itself, if one object is said to be the same as itself, or as between two objects, if they are said to be the same, there can be as many kinds of sameness as there are kinds of division or distinction. This is according to the principle: The predicates proper to one of a pair of opposites correspond in number to the predicates proper to the other. Hence things can be really the same, modally the same, and the same according to the reasoned reason. As for the reasoning reason, there is nothing that cannot be distinguished from itself, if it is compared with itself in some way. However, if a thing is in no sense conceived as plural, it will in no sense be some things, but only something. Hence Aristotle says, in the passage cited,[65] that sameness is a certain unity either of more than one thing, or of one thing when it is treated as more than one. Some things are the same really and modally, but not in concept; other things can be the same really, but not modally; still others are in no sense the same in reality, but only according to concept.

From this we can understand how "the same" and "other" are opposed. They are opposed, first, with respect to the same thing, not with respect to other things, since they are opposed after the fashion of relatives. Secondly, they are opposed as compared with the same kind of distinction or division. For a negation will not be opposed to an affirmation unless it is predicated of the same thing according to the same respect; but these predicates are opposed inasmuch as one involves a

---

[63] E.g., in Disp. VI, sect. 2, nos. 9-14; sect. 5, no. 2.
[64] Disp. XLVII, *passim;* e.g. sect. 1, nos. 10, 12; sect. 3, nos. 2-5; 10-13; sect. 9, no. 3.
[65] *Metaphysica,* V, 9, 1018a 7-9. Junta, VIII, text 16, fol. 56 rb. 14-17.

denial of the other. Therefore to be really the same excludes being really other, but does not exclude being other modally or mentally. Conversely, to be the same in concept does not exclude being really distinct or other, because reason unifies in concept things that are really other, just as, on the contrary, it distinguishes in concept things that are really the same; this is clear from what was said above on universal unity.[66]

5. The objection may be raised that although not every identity involves a negation of all diversity, a greater identity seems to argue the negation of a greater diversity. Thus, if some things are the same modally, we not only infer that they are not modally other, but also that they are not really other. Therefore, since sameness in concept is seemingly the greatest of all, modal and real sameness are rightly inferred from it.

I answer that an equivocation in the term, sameness of concept, occurs here. This sameness is not always the greatest. There is, indeed, a kind of sameness in concept which reason does not make, but merely recognizes; and this is the greatest, for it supposes not only actual negation of a distinction in the object, but also the negation of a foundation for a distinction, that is, the negation of a virtual distinction. But there is another conceptual sameness, which reason makes, and this is not the greatest. In fact it is only a sameness in a qualified sense, since it does not simply suppose sameness in the object, but only a foundation for likeness or conformity. Accordingly such unity does not simply exclude diversity in the real order.

6. *The meaning of "to be distinct", "to differ", and "to be other"; comparison of these concepts.* Here we must avoid equivocation in the terms "to be distinct", "to differ", and "to be other". In his *Metaphysics*, Bk. V, chap. 9, and Bk. X, chap. 5,[67] Aristotle points out that "to differ" and "to be other" are not equivalent. For things are said to differ when they agree in some detail and are distinct in another; but they are said to be other when they do not agree in any respect. Hence "to be other" seems to imply more than "to differ", as Aristotle again remarks in Bk. IV, chap. 2.[68] It is in this sense that we here understand "to be other". But "to be distinct" is sometimes understood in the same sense as "to be other", although in another and rather common acceptation, "to be distinct" seems only to imply the denial of real identity, whereas "to be other" seems to add the denial of likeness and conformity. Thus one picture is said to be distinct from another, although they are similar; but if it is said to be other, apparently this signifies not merely that it is distinct, but further that it is unlike, or less perfect.

---

[66] In Disp. VI; see especially the references given in note 63.
[67] *Metaphysica*, V, 9, 1018a 9-13, Junta VIII, text 16, fol. 56 rb 18-24; X, 6, 1056b 34-1057a 1, Junta, VIII, text 20, fol. 126 ra 8-13.
[68] *Metaphysica*, IV, 2, 1004a 12-16. Junta, VIII, text 3, fol. 32 va 13-20

But, as I have stated, all this regards only the meaning of the terms, for the matter itself is quite clear. Consequently, for "the same" and "other" to be opposed, they must be understood with comparison and reference to the same object; thus they imply an immediate opposition, like "one" and "many", as Aristotle says in *Metaphysics,* Bk. IV, chap. 2,[69] since one includes the negation of the other.

7. Hence we can see how every being is the same or other with regard to everything else, as Aristotle expressly states, *Metaphysics,* Bk. X, chap. 5.[70] On this Soncinas has much to say, in his commentary on this text, qq. 5 and 6; also Javelli, qq. 7 and 8. The point is easily understood. If the two predicates are taken relatively, they do not have to apply to every being, for a mental relation is not necessary, as is self-evident, nor does one being always require another to which it may be really referred with a real relation of identity or diversity, as is evident in God. Of course in creatures, which essentially depend on God, there will always be a real relation of diversity or distinction, if there is question of a real relation. But if we speak of fundamental or negative sameness (as in fact we should), or of sameness with regard to diverse aspects, every being is the same as itself, and is diverse from every other being, whether actual or possible, or even from fictitious or imaginary being. For of any of these we can deny, in the terminology favored by many, that something *(aliquid)* is a passion of being, seeing that it signifies no more than division from everything else. But with respect to one and the same thing, every being is either the same as it or other than it, if these predicates are understood as parallels, for thus they involve a contradiction. The case is otherwise if the kinds of identity or diversity vary, as is clear from this whole discussion.

You may say: man and animal are neither the same nor other, because they pertain neither to the same genus or species, nor to another. For they neither come together in an ultimate differentia, and hence cannot be of the same species, nor do they have opposite ultimate differentiae, which would enable them to differ in species.

I reply that "the same" and "other" are directly opposed with regard to the same aspect, if they are understood as negative or privative opposites, but not if they are understood as contraries. Thus in the present case, if "to be other" in species is taken merely in a quasi-negative sense, genus and species, or man and animal, can be said to be other in ultimate species, because they are not constituted by the same ultimate differentia. But if "to be other" in species is understood as it were positively and in a contrary sense, then they are neither the same in species nor

---

[69] *Ibid.,* 1005a 4-5. Junta, VIII, text 6, fol. 33 vb 58-59.
[70] *Ibid.,* X, 3, 1054b 25. Junta, VIII, text 12, fol. 122 rb 7-8.

do they differ in species. In parallel fashion they are neither the same nor other in genus. Negatively, however, since they do not come together immediately in the same genus, they may be said not to belong to the same genus. So when we say that these predicates are immediately opposed, one of the extremes is to be taken negatively.

Hence, also, to be opposed to another is considered a passion of being, not indeed by relative opposition, which would require both extremes, but by fundamental opposition, inasmuch as every being has in itself some aspect, differentia, or essence which excludes from it every opposed or contradictory aspect, differentia, or essence. But this is to be understood of opposition in the wide sense, as comprising not only the four classes listed by Aristotle in the *Categories* and in the fifth and tenth books of the *Metaphysics*,[71] but any kind of contrariety. Or certainly it can be understood of the foundation of opposition; for this is enough to constitute at least a contradiction, with respect to any other being whatsoever. Accordingly no more is explained by the term "opposition" than by the term "diversity". But this is a sufficient treatment of this property of being.

8. *Explanation of an Aristotelian dictum.* Finally, we can gather from the foregoing doctrine the meaning of an axiom enunciated by Aristotle in the fourth book of the *Metaphysics:*[72] Things which are the same as a third thing, are the same as each other. Due proportion must be observed in applying this principle. If two things are in reality identical with a third thing, they will also be identical with each other in reality, although they may be diverse in concept. And if they are identical with a third thing both in reality and in concept, they will be identical with each other in the same way. In creatures and in finite things this principle avails absolutely. But in an infinite thing, such as is the divine essence, the maxim is not verified, absolutely speaking, since on account of its infinity the divine essence can be identical with opposite relations which, because of this opposition, cannot be identical with one another, except in the essence alone. But we have dealt with this problem on another occasion.[73]

---

[71] *Categoriae*, 10, 11b 17-19, Junta, I, fol. 26 vb 7-15: *Metaphysica*, V. 10, 1018ᵃ 20-22. Junta, VIII, text 16, fol. 56 rb. 36-38; *Metaphysica* X, 3, 1054a 23-24, Junta VIII, text 9, fol. 121 ra 67-68.
[72] See note 56.
[73] *De Sanctissimo Trinitatis mysterio*, Lib. IV, cap. 3; in Vol. I of the Vivès edition.